★TOP★ SECRET

DATA ENCRYPTION TECHNIQUES

★ TOP ★ SECRET

DATA ENCRYPTION TECHNIQUES

Gilbert Held

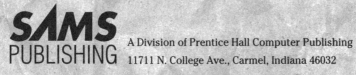

SAMS PUBLISHING

A Division of Prentice Hall Computer Publishing

11711 N. College Ave., Carmel, Indiana 46032

This book is dedicated to those people in the National Security Agency whose work cannot be told but whose efforts are truly appreciated.

© 1993 BY SAMS PUBLISHING

FIRST EDITION

International Standard Book Number: 0-672-30293-4

Library of Congress Catalog Card Number: 92-83921

96 95 94 93   4 3 2 1

Interpretation of the printing code: the rightmost double-digit number is the year of the book's printing; the rightmost single-digit, the number of the book's printing. For example, a printing code of 93-1 shows that the first printing of the book occurred in 1993.

TRADEMARKS

Composed in MCPdigital, Cheltenham, and Stencil by Prentice Hall Computer Publishing

Printed in the United States of America

Publisher
Richard K. Swadley

Acquisitions Manager
Jordan Gold

Acquisitions Editor
Gregg Bushyeager

Development Editor
Phillip W. Paxton

Senior Editor
Grant Fairchild

Production Editor
Grant Fairchild

Editorial Coordinator
Rebecca S. Freeman

Editorial Assistant
Rosemarie Graham

Technical Editor
Ray Sarch

Cover Designer
Tim Amrhein

**Director of Production
and Manufacturing**
Jeff Valler

Production Manager
Corinne Walls

Imprint Manager
Matthew Morrill

Book Designer
Amy Peppler-Adams

Production Analyst
Mary Beth Wakefield

**Proofreading/Indexing
Coordinator**
Joelynn Gifford

Graphics Image Specialists
Dennis Sheehan
Jerry Ellis
Sue VandeWalle

Production
Christine Cook
Carla Hall-Batton
John Kane
Juli Pavey
Michelle M. Self
Greg Simsic
Angie Trzepacz

Indexers
Loren Malloy
Suzanne Snyder

OVERVIEW

CONTENTS

3 Keyword-Based Monoalphabetic Substitution   59

4 Transposition-Based Monoalphabetic Substitution   83

PREFACE

"Bid $3.62 million on the 46th Street project," "potential corporate acquisition requires suspension of training activities through the end of month," and "meet me at 7 p.m. in the Raddison lobby to discuss . . ." are a few examples of personal communication that for one reason or another should be confidential.

We live in a world whose "communications dimensions" have rapidly shrunk due to the explosive growth in the use of computer-based networks. Messages that took hours or days to reach a recipient a decade ago are now delivered practically instantaneously to most areas of the globe. Although advances in communication technology have considerably enhanced our quality of life, it has also provided the con artist, the computer hacker, and persons many would classify as belonging in the lower elements of society with the ability to electronically take advantage of others. An unscrupulous person may commit electronic fraud by ordering items and billing the cost to others, read personal messages, and take actions that are harmful to other people. In other situations, the inadvertent viewing of a personal message concerning a potential corporate reorganization, pending personnel action, or similar activity can result in an exponential increase in the rumor mill—employee productivity often decreases in an inverse proportion to these rumors.

Although it is doubtful that fraud or rumors will ever cease as long as humans populate the earth, there are steps you can take to keep personal communications personal. Some steps, such as routing messages correctly, avoid the embarrassment of an unintentional recipient. Other steps, such as converting your message into a sequence of characters that is not meaningful to an unintended recipient or casual observer, provide a mechanism to protect the content of your message. It is this area that

is the focus of this book, which provides practical methods readers can use to obtain a degree of privacy and security for messages that are transmitted over internal corporate communications networks or public electronic messaging systems.

The focus of this book is use of cryptology to encipher and decipher messages. Encipherment methods, as well as the development of programs written in the BASIC programming language that can be used to automate the encipherment and decipherment process are also examined. The techniques covered in this book are available to everyone—the techniques discussed in this book are in the public domain.

Most techniques covered in this book are based upon the use of keywords, phrases, or the selection of a random sequence of characters. Although almost any enciphering technique can be broken, given a long enough message and time, the objective of this book is to provide readers with a mechanism to prevent the inadvertent reading of messages and to delay the translation of messages intercepted by hackers, rascals, and scoundrels—a message concerning a bid due on Tuesday may be worthless to a person who reads the contents of your message on Thursday.

To illustrate this point with my wallet, I am offering a reward to readers of this book! The first person to successfully decipher the message contained in the last chapter of this book will receive $1,000. The message you need to decipher was enciphered using a program contained on the convenience disk accompanying this book and can be deciphered using a decipherment program which is also contained on the convenience disk. The use of both programs is described in the final chapter of this book. By carefully considering the use of different enciphering techniques and keywords, phrases, or random character sequences to govern the encipherment process, you can keep personal communications personal and obtain a degree of message security that will enable you to conduct your business in a more efficient and effective manner.

As a professional author, I consider reader feedback extremely important, and I encourage you to send me your comments. Let me know if the information and techniques presented in this book satisfied your requirements or if there are other areas you would like me to tackle in a future edition. You can write to me directly or contact me through Sams Publishing. Send your comments to:

Gilbert Held
4736 Oxford Road
Macon, GA 31210

ACKNOWLEDGMENTS

From proposal to publication, a book requires the efforts of many individuals besides the author. Because I spend a majority of my writing time at home, the cooperation and assistance of my family is essential and once again is greatly appreciated.

As an old-fashioned author, I like to write my manuscript and depend upon the professional skills of Mrs. Carol Ferrell to turn my longhand notes and diagrams into a suitable manuscript. Thus, once again I am also indebted to Carol Ferrell for her fine work.

While many persons can write manuscripts, only a select few have the ability and position to judge the viability of a book proposal, arrange for the editing of a manuscript, and coordinate the thousand and one items (from the cover design to the production schedule) that enable the finished product to reach the market. It is with sincere appreciation that I thank Mr. Gregg Bushyeager for his cooperation and assistance as well as his vision and foresight in noting the role of this book in fulfilling the requirements of readers.

ABOUT
THE AUTHOR

Gilbert Held is an internationally recognized author and lecturer who specializes in the application of computer and communications technology. The author of more than 20 books about personal computers, data communications, and business topics, Held is the only person to twice receive the coveted Interface Karp Award and an award from the American Publisher's Institute.

Held currently manages a nationwide data communications network for the federal government. This network supports one of the largest number of dial-in data encryption devices in use throughout the free world. Held is a frequent lecturer and often conducts seminars on such topics as LAN and WAN internetworking, data compression, and personal computer hardware and software.

TECHNOLOGY AND TERMINOLOGY

★ TOP ★ SECRET

1

The primary purpose of this chapter is to acquaint you with a core set of terms associated with the field of cryptology. You should note that your primary objective is to develop and use practical encipherment techniques to hide the meaning of messages transmitted over different types of electronic mail systems. Many of the techniques covered in this book are not unbreakable to a trained analyst. These techniques, however, provide varying levels of message protection that can make it difficult and, in many cases, very time-consuming to understand the meaning of a message. In fact, some practical techniques covered in this book may require more than 60 billion trials to correctly understand the meaning of a message. Because each trial could require the printing of an intercepted message, a 10-line message could conceivably require a person to scan 600 billion printed lines!

Although the United States National Security Agency (NSA), the United Kingdom's MI5, and Russia's KGB have probably programmed supercomputers to use artificial intelligence in an

attempt to understand the meaning of intercepted messages, few, if any, commercial organizations have the financial resources to obtain the required hardware to develop programs that perform similar operations. Thus, the more sophisticated techniques presented in this book should provide you with a mechanism to protect the meaning of your communications from the casual observer, the inadvertent observer, and most, if not all, intentional illicit intercepters.

To acquaint you with the terminology associated with the field of cryptology, terms, their meanings, and examples are presented in this chapter. The main types of ciphers are discussed and covered in detail in succeeding chapters. When appropriate, the historical basis of ciphers is also discussed. The intention here, however, is not to provide you with information on the historical evolution of ciphers but to show you some of their practical uses from a historical basis.

The secondary objective of this chapter is to discuss the subroutines and programs developed and included in program listings in this book. This discussion will acquaint you with the rationale for selecting the BASIC language that is used to develop subroutines, programs, and filenaming conventions which can facilitate the use of the subroutines and programs included in this book.

CIPHERS VERSUS CODES

One of the major areas of confusion about this subject is the difference between a cipher system and a code system. Although both systems are designed to conceal information during transmission, they do so using different substitution techniques.

If you're a video buff and remember The Longest Day, Tora, Tora, Tora, *and other war films, you may have noticed that seemingly meaningless messages were often transmitted— "Paul has a long arm," "The soup is in the kitchen," and "Ralph needs shoes," for example, represent coded messages in which words and phrases are substituted for other words or phrases to disguise the meaning of the message. In other films, you may remember a soldier or sailor using equipment to intercept a message and preparing a punched paper tape containing the contents of the message. The paper tape was then placed into a special tape reader that read the tape and produced a new tape. The soldier or sailor would then read the message on the new tape and yell across the room, "Let's get this message to the Captain."*

Those movies illustrated the use of specially constructed decipherment machines designed to read enciphered messages and reproduce the original text of the message, known as plaintext *or* cleartext. *The intercepted message punched on paper tape consisted of a series of what appeared to be randomly picked characters, such as the sequence QAFRT. That character sequence represented an enciphered message in which each plaintext character in the message was replaced by a ciphertext character according to a predefined algorithm.*

In a cipher system, plaintext, which represents a set of data prior to encipherment, is operated on without regard to meaning. In a code system, words or phrases are replaced by other words or phrases to hide the meaning of a message. Thus, the message FIRE THE CORPORATE LAWYER might be transmitted as GJSF UIF OPSQPSBUF MBXZFS using a simple cipher (discussed later in this chapter). When transmitted in a code, the message could become SELL THE CORPORATE DONKEY, assuming SELL was the code for FIRE and DONKEY was the code for LAWYER.

Because many code systems normally do not change the meaning of more than a few terms in a message, such systems immediately provide a hint as to the contents of the message. In addition, the observation of a series of messages can provide a reasonable set of clues that may enable someone to determine the meaning of coded messages. Another obstacle to the use of codes, especially when they are only used infrequently, is the requirement of prior knowledge of all substitutions. Some code systems used by military and diplomatic personnel are based on the creation of code books that may contain tens of thousands of terms and their equivalent codes. Not only are such code books difficult and time-consuming to prepare, but their distribution and replacement (if an existing book is lost or compromised) can create a logistical nightmare.

Many cipher systems, however, only require knowledge of one or a few items of information known as *keys* to encipher and decipher a message. From a practical point of view, encipherment and decipherment operations can be easier to perform than encoding and decoding operations, especially as the length of a message increases. In addition, many cipher systems can be expected to provide a higher level of message protection than a code system. Thus, the focus of this book: encipherment techniques.

CIPHER TERMINOLOGY

As previously described, a cipher system is a system in which a substitution process occurs on individual characters or groups of characters without regard to meaning. The actual enciphering process can be performed by hardware, software, or brainpower (manually).

PLAINTEXT AND ENCIPHERED TEXT

The use of a cipher system requires a message or text on which to operate. The original, unaltered contents of the message or text is known as plaintext or cleartext. Through the use of a

cipher system, the meaning of the plaintext message is hidden. The process of hiding the meaning of the plaintext is known as enciphering, and the resulting text is referred to as enciphered text.

ENCIPHERMENT

Figure 1.1 illustrates the encipherment process in a block diagram format. Note that plaintext (x) is converted to ciphertext (y) by an enciphering process (E) so that $y=Ek(x)$, where k is a key. The enciphering process can be considered as an algorithm that operates on the plaintext based on the value of a key (k). Thus, the key defines the operation of the encipherment algorithm, and different keys produce different ciphertext from a fixed plaintext.

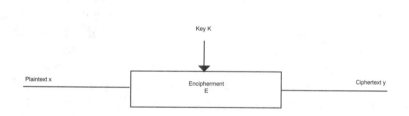

Figure 1.1.
The encipherment process results in the creation of ciphertext (y) by applying an encipherment algorithm (E) controlled by a key (k) against plaintext so that y=Ek(x).

DECIPHERMENT

The process of converting or restoring ciphertext to its original plaintext contents is known as *decipherment*. Figure 1.2 illustrates the decipherment process in a block diagram format. Decipherment (D) can be considered the inverse of the encipherment process, requiring the use of an algorithm that converts ciphertext back into its original plaintext. Decipherment is also controlled by a key (k), which is applied to ciphertext (y) to produce plaintext (x) so that $x=Dk(y)$.

Figure 1.2.
The decipherment process results in the creation of plaintext (x) by applying a decipherment algorithm (D) controlled by a key (k) against ciphertext (y) so that x=Dk(y).

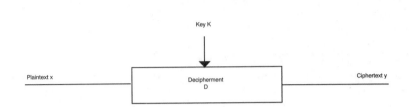

KEYS AND KEY SPACE

In Figure 1.1 and 1.2, the key—no pun intended—to enciphering and deciphering is the key that controls the operation of the enciphering and deciphering algorithms. Although you may obtain a copy of an enciphered message and have knowledge of the algorithm used to encipher the message, you must use the correct key to successfully decipher the message. Thus, the number of possible values of a key, referred to as an algorithm's *key space*, is an important consideration when selecting an enciphering algorithm—an algorithm with a limited key space is very susceptible to a trial-and-error process in which different keys are applied in an attempt to decipher an intercepted message. If a sequence of nine decimal digits, for example, is used to form a key, its key space is 10^{10}, or 10 billion, key values.

Although it is relatively easy to program a computer to generate a series of 10-digit sequences to use at different times, it is probably not realistic to expect a mortal to remember those sequences. Thus, a tradeoff occurs between key space and practicality if you wish to develop ciphers that can be easily used in a manual process. From a practical point of view, it is much easier to remember words or phrases than a sequence of

digits. Many of the cipher systems discussed in this book are based on the use of an alphabetic key in the form of a word or phrase. This usually provides an increased retention capability for a digit sequence. Even if you automate the enciphering process through the use of a program executed on a personal computer, in certain situations you may prefer to use a word or phrase in place of a digit sequence to facilitate the use of the program.

Another reason for using alphabetic or alphanumeric keys instead of a key restricted to digits is the significant increase in the key space afforded by the use of alphabetic or alphanumeric keys. A two-digit key, for example, provides 10*10, or 100, unique keys. In comparison, the use of two uppercase or two lowercase alphabetic characters in a key provides 26*26, or 676, unique keys, and the use of two alphanumeric characters in which alphabetic characters are limited to a single case produces 36*36, or 1,296, unique keys.

Table 1.1 contains the key space obtained by the use of digits, letters, and alphanumeric characters for keys varying in length from 1 to 20 positions. The field width column indicates the number of characters in a key. You should note that the discussion of key space is limited to the use of all uppercase or all lowercase letters when alphabetic or alphanumeric keys are used (unless otherwise noted). Although the use of both uppercase and lowercase letters significantly increases the key space, it also increases the potential for confusion. That is, it is quite easy to remember a word or phrase and easy to forget which letters are uppercase and which letters are lowercase. For this reason, the use of keys in this book is usually restricted to letters of a single case. If the key is limited to eight positions and you wish to use the word "computer," enter the key as "COMPUTER" or "computer," but not as "Computer," unless you develop a program that is case-insensitive and converts all characters to one case.

Table 1.1.
Key space based on characters used and field width.

Field Width	Digit Combinations	Letter Combinations	Alphanumeric Combinations
1	1.00000E+01	2.60000E+01	3.60000E+01
2	1.00000E+02	6.76000E+02	1.29600E+03
3	1.00000E+03	1.75760E+04	4.66560E+04
4	1.00000E+04	4.56976E+05	1.67962E+06
5	1.00000E+05	1.18814E+07	6.04662E+02
6	1.00000E+06	3.08916E+08	2.17678E+09
7	1.00000E+07	8.03181E+09	7.83642E+10
8	1.00000E+08	2.08827E+11	2.82111E+12
9	1.00000E+09	5.42950E+12	1.01560E+14
10	1.00000E+10	1.41167E+14	3.65616E+15
11	1.00000E+11	3.67034E+15	1.31622E+17
12	1.00000E+12	9.54290E+16	4.73838E+18
13	1.00000E+13	2.48115E+18	1.70582E+20
14	1.00000E+14	6.45100E+19	6.14094E+21
15	1.00000E+15	1.67726E+21	2.21074E+23
16	1.00000E+16	4.36087E+22	7.95866E+24
17	1.00000E+17	1.13383E+24	2.86512E+26
18	1.00000E+18	2.94795E+25	1.03144E+28
19	1.00000E+19	7.66467E+26	3.71319E+29
20	1.00000E+20	1.99281E+28	1.33675E+31

In examining the entries in Table 1.1, you should note that E+6 represents one million and E+9 represents one billion. Thus, a six-character alphanumeric field produces 2.17 billion combinations even when the alphabet is restricted to all uppercase or all lowercase letters! You should also note that a nine-character field is required to obtain just one billion key combinations if the key is restricted to digits. Thus, you can maintain a large key space with a lesser number of key characters or increase your key space by using alphanumeric characters instead of restricting your key to digits or letters.

KEY GENERATION, MANAGEMENT, AND DISTRIBUTION

An enciphering system that produces billions of possible key combinations may be extremely vulnerable if keys are selected in a manner in which their possible composition can be easily guessed. A birth date or home address, for example, would not be advisable for use as a key because these examples represent the most common trials in a trial-and-error process an unauthorized person may attempt to use as a key. Ideally, keys should be generated based on some random process. However, if you're traveling and wish to use your laptop or notebook computer to transmit or receive private messages enciphered according to a predefined key, you would probably prefer to remember PCATV instead of Q4R51. Because PCATV is obviously an easier guess than Q4R51, use a random process to generate keys and then store those keys for use over a predefined period of time on a computer file enciphered using a different key. In this case, employees need only to remember one key (for a period of time) to access a list of keys and the period of time each key is valid. This technique is one of many methods associated with key management.

Key management can be considered the process of generating, maintaining, and distributing keys. This activity is responsible for defining what action or actions to take in the event a cipher system or key to a cipher system is lost or compromised.

The key management process, as well as functions associated with this process, vary from organization to organization based on a variety of factors (the number of employees that require knowledge of an enciphering key, their geographical distribution, and the integrity of the firm's internal mail service). Some organizations deliver cipher keys via internal interoffice mail in a manner similar to the distribution of computer passwords. Other organizations distribute keys through registered mail, a corporate electronic mail system enciphered using the current key, or in plaintext. Obviously, the repeated distribution of new keys in plaintext or those enciphered using the currently-in-use

key opens the organization to a potentially compromising situation. However, you should remember that many organizations simply want a mechanism to keep personal communications personal—they are not looking for, nor do they seek, an elaborate method to guarantee that their communications are never broken. Although some sophisticated methods to distribute keys are discussed in succeeding chapters, the primary focus of attention in this book is placed on practical and efficient methods to distribute keys.

Regardless of the manner in which new keys are distributed, they should be distributed because employees will leave the organization, lose their keys, misplace a message containing a listing of keys, and do other things that can compromise a system.

Perhaps one of the more interesting public compromises of security occurred when a president of the United States was photographed with a document folded in his suit pocket. The document was folded in such a manner that a keyword was prominently displayed in the photograph that appeared in newspapers. Fortunately for national security, the keyword denoted a classification associated with a special type of communications and did not reflect the key used to encipher communications. Unfortunately for many people involved in national security, the display of the keyword resulted in a large amount of unpaid overtime required to rapidly change the keyword used to classify the type of communications that was exposed to the public.

At some federal agencies, keys are changed on a quarterly basis. Other agencies change keys on a monthly, weekly, and even a daily basis. The driving force behind the frequency of key changes should be the worth of the data and the potential threat to that data. The threat may be hard to judge because most

people don't know that their electronic conversations are targeted for interception until it is too late. In addition to the potential threat, you must balance key changes against the effort required to develop and distribute new keys on a periodic basis. If the system you devise is difficult to implement or requires too much effort to effectively use, many potential users may bypass the system you develop. The old military adage— keep it simple—is worth remembering when you consider various methods for the generation and distribution of keys.

TYPES OF CIPHERS

A visit to a large university or public library will reward you with the ability to locate a large number of books about the use of cipher systems. Some books, such as *The Codebreakers* (Macmillan, 1969) by David Kahn and *Cryptanalysis* (Dover Publications, 1956) by Helen F. Gaines, provide an excellent overview of a variety of cipher systems, primarily focusing on the historical use of such systems. More recently published works, such as *Security for Computer Networks* by D. W. Davies and W. L. Price, can bring you up-to-date on recent developments in the construction of cipher systems from a mathematical basis.

These and other books will acquaint you with hundreds of types of cipher systems, ranging in scope from an elementary process that can be performed mentally to very complex systems that require the use of a computer. What each of these cipher systems has in common is the ability to be classified into one of two general categories: substitution and transposition. The remainder of this section focuses on an initial overview of each cipher category and provides a discussion of several of the variants used to develop specific types of cipher systems. This is followed by a discussion of the constraints that must be recognized when considering the algorithms and the key space used to convert plaintext to ciphertext for use with many electronic mail systems.

SUBSTITUTION CIPHER SYSTEMS

In a substitution cipher system, each plaintext character is replaced by a ciphertext character using an algorithm that operates on plaintext in the sequence in which the plaintext characters appear. In a simple substitution cipher system, the replacement process is unaltered—each plaintext character is replaced by the same ciphertext character. For example, the well-known Caesar Cipher, in which the ciphertext represents a fixed displacement in the alphabet, would encipher the message KILL ALL THE LAWYERS as LJMM BMM UIF MBXZFST using a displacement of one character position as the encipherment algorithm.

You can denote the relationship between a plaintext alphabet and a ciphertext alphabet by listing one alphabet above the other. For example, restrict your plaintext and ciphertext alphabets to the 26 uppercase letters. Then, for the simple one-character Caesar Cipher displacement, the relationship between the plaintext alphabet (P) and the ciphertext alphabet (C) is as appears in the following example. In this example, the letters in the ciphertext alphabet are displaced by one character position from the letters in the plaintext alphabet. You can denote this relationship between the mapping of plaintext and ciphertext characters as $P_A = C_B$, which indicates that the letter A in the plaintext alphabet is aligned with the letter B in the ciphertext alphabet.

Plaintext alphabet (P):   ABCDEFGHIJKLMNOPQRSTUVWXYZ

Ciphertext alphabet (C):   BCDEFGHIJKLMNOPQRSTUVWXYZA

In a varying substitution cipher, the replacement of plaintext by ciphertext results in a very high probability that repeating plaintext characters are replaced by different ciphertext characters. To accomplish this you must use more than one "mapping" alphabet to convert plaintext to ciphertext—a term referred to as *polyalphabetic substitution*. As an alternative, a random or pseudorandom sequence can be used to generate a variable ciphertext replacement. Varying substitutions through the use

of a pseudorandom sequence generated by a key is the basis for many commercially developed enciphering systems as well as the well-known data encryption standard (DES). In separate chapters in this book the construction of monoalphabetic, polyalphabetic, and pseudorandom number-based cipher systems are examined.

Prior to the start of World War II, the U.S. Army Signal Corps successfully constructed a cipher machine called PURPLE that duplicated the cryptographic operations of a Japanese machine. Intercepted Japanese transmissions were fed into PURPLE to produce plaintext information that was then translated into English and distributed under the code name MAGIC to President Roosevelt and top-level civilian and military officials within his administration. Although a series of urgent messages from Tokyo to the Japanese ambassador in Washington was intercepted and deciphered, this secret effort did not prevent the Pearl Harbor attack simply because Japan never transmitted a message stating they would attack Pearl Harbor! Whether intentional or not, the lack of an explicit attack message resulted in a degree of complacency within the U.S. government. The ability to read enciphered messages, although important, does not necessarily mean you will always be able to understand the intentions of others. Effective in many situations, the ability to read enciphered messages is no substitute for the analysis of the contents of those messages. In June of 1942, for example, U.S. Naval Intelligence decoding of intercepted Japanese transmissions noted that one Japanese unit gave Midway as its post office address. By concentrating U.S. Naval forces to meet the Japanese threat, the Battle of Midway represented the turning point of the war in the Pacific.

TRANSPOSITION CIPHER SYSTEMS

As its name implies, a transposition cipher system rearranges the characters in a message. An elementary transposition

system could simply swap plaintext character positions so that position n is mapped to $n+1$ and position $n+1$ is mapped to position n. In this case, the message KILL ALL THE LAWYERS becomes IKLL LAT LEH ALYWRES. (In the preceding example, note that a visual observation immediately provides a good clue as to the meaning of the plaintext.)

As an alternative to the transposition of plaintext characters, some cipher systems are based on the use of an algorithm that transposes the characters of a mapping alphabet or series of mapping alphabets. A variety of transposition systems are covered in a later chapter of this book.

ELECTRONIC MAIL TRANSMISSION CONSIDERATIONS

Up to this point, I have simply glossed over the contents of the plaintext alphabet and the resulting ciphertext alphabet. The plaintext alphabet represents all possible characters in the character set used to develop a plaintext message. The ciphertext alphabet represents all possible enciphered characters resulting from the enciphering process. It is the plaintext character set and the enciphering process that generates the ciphertext character set you must consider to successfully transmit an enciphered message through many electronic mail systems. The reason for this is the fact that most computer alphabets use eight bits to represent a character. This results in 2^8, or 256, unique characters that can be used to represent both plaintext and ciphertext alphabet sets. Unfortunately, several electronic mail systems are restricted to transmitting seven-bit characters (with the eighth bit in a transmitted byte used for parity). Such electronic mail systems are restricted to transmitting 2^7, or 128, characters. This means that many cipher systems, such as the DES algorithm, that are not restricted with respect to the generated ciphertext alphabet cannot be used to transfer data across certain electronic mail systems.

To obtain the capability to transmit ciphertext via certain electronic mail systems you need to place limits on both the plaintext alphabet set and the algorithm used to create ciphertext. Several methods you can use to limit the plaintext alphabet set and the algorithm used to generate a ciphertext alphabet are discussed at appropriate points in succeeding chapters.

SUBROUTINES AND PROGRAMS

To extend the practical use of encipherment, numerous routines are developed in this book to perform different enciphering- and deciphering-related operations. To provide code that can be utilized by a maximum number of readers, Microsoft Corporation's QuickBASIC compiler was used to develop the subroutines and programs contained in this book.

QuickBASIC was selected for several reasons. First and foremost, every version of PC-DOS and MS-DOS contains a BASIC language interpreter on the DOS distribution disk. This means that most readers can easily adapt the subroutines and programs presented in this book to execute through the use of a BASIC language interpreter at no additional cost. You can use the programs as is, modify one or more programs, or select a number of subroutines that can be viewed similarly to a construction set for the design of a program tailored to your requirements.

The second reason for the selection of QuickBASIC is the availability of QBASIC on all DOS distribution disks (commencing with release 5.0). QBASIC can execute all subroutines and programs presented in this book without modification. Other reasons for the selection of QuickBASIC include the large number of people knowledgeable in BASIC programming and the ability of the compiler to produce object code.

The large number of people familiar with BASIC programming enables more people to put theory into practice. The capability of the compiler to produce object code permitted the inclusion

of read-to-run, executable program files on the convenience disk. This allows you to directly execute a program without having to modify the source code (this is required if a BASIC interpreter is used). Of course, you cannot modify the executable program, which may take some of the fun out of the use of the program if you would like to attempt to modify one or more functions.

FILENAMING CONVENTIONS

To facilitate the use of the convenience disk, a set of filenaming conventions was developed and used to reference program listings in this book as well as files on the convenience disk. Files with the extension .BAS are BASIC language source code files. In this book, these files appear as subroutine and program listings. Files with the extension .DAT reference data files. These files contain plaintext and ciphertext messages that demonstrate the operation and utilization of the programs developed in this book (they are also contained on the convenience disk). The third type of file has the extension .EXE. Files with this extension represent executable programs that you can directly run on any DOS-based personal computer. Refer to the Appendix for a list of files (including names and descriptions) contained on the convenience disk.

2

MONOALPHABETIC SUBSTITUTION CONCEPTS

At first glance, the title of this chapter may evoke a vision of coverage of a medical disease. The focus in this chapter is on the use of single letters or characters contained in one alphabet to replace plaintext letters and characters in a message. Because replacement letters and characters are restricted to those included in one alphabet, the term *monoalphabet* is employed. In recognition of the fact that characters in the alphabet are substituted for plaintext characters, the encipherment process is referred to as a monoalphabetic substitution process.

In some books you may have seen the term *uniliteral substitution* or *monoalphabetic uniliteral substitution*. The word *uniliteral* denotes the fact that the replacement process occurs on a character-by-character basis with one character from the replacement alphabet substituted for each character in the plaintext message.

EVOLUTION

Monoalphabetic uniliteral substitution represents one of the earliest methods of cryptology—the technique employed by Julius Caesar approximately 20 centuries ago to hide the contents of messages he sent by courier. Although Caesar's method of encipherment was relatively elementary, his name has been associated with a class of displacement enciphering techniques, and the term *Caesar cipher* is used to denote encipherment by displacement.

According to historical records, Caesar wrote to Cicero and other friends using a cipher system in which the plaintext letters in his message were replaced by letters three positions further down the alphabet. Thus, in the English language, INVADE would be enciphered as LQYDGH and ENGLAND would be enciphered as HQJODQG.

Augustus Caesar, the nephew of Julius and first emperor of Rome, modified his uncle's technique. Augustus substituted for each plaintext character, reducing the displacement from three positions to one. Whether Augustus had difficulty in counting, arthritis (which precluded counting by the use of his fingers), or just wanted to make deciphering easier is unknown. What is known is that any enciphering system in which plaintext characters are replaced by characters in an alphabet displaced from the plaintext alphabet is referred to as a Caesar cipher, and the displaced alphabet is called a Caesar alphabet.

Although a Caesar cipher is a rather elementary enciphering technique, it provided a foundation for the development of more advanced monoalphabetic substitution techniques. An understanding of that class of ciphers provides you with the ability to recognize the advantages and disadvantages of other techniques whose foundations can be traced to the Caesar cipher.

Prior to examining the use of uniliteral substitution systems, the definition of a few terms that will be used throughout this chapter may be helpful. I'll restrict the alphabet to the upper-case letters A through Z and ignore lowercase letters, punctuation characters, and numerics for simplicity of illustration (numerics and punctuation characters can be spelled out— ZERO, COMMA, and so on). In fact, in many military systems the English alphabet is restricted to the 26 uppercase characters. However, you can easily expand the examples presented in this chapter to incorporate the use of larger character sets.

ALPHABETS

There are two basic types of alphabets you must consider when developing a monoalphabetic uniliteral substitution system— a plaintext alphabet and a ciphertext alphabet. The plaintext alphabet represents the alphabet from which the characters of a message are constructed; the ciphertext alphabet represents the sequence of characters used to replace the plaintext characters during the uniliteral substitution process. Because the characters in the ciphertext alphabet replace the characters in the plaintext alphabet, the ciphertext alphabet is also commonly known as a substitution alphabet.

ALPHABETIC RELATIONSHIPS

The top portion of the following example illustrates the elementary relationship between a direct-sequence plaintext alphabet and a direct-sequence ciphertext alphabet. In this example, the ciphertext alphabet was shifted or wrapped five character positions to the right of the plaintext alphabet if the wraparound of each character is considered to represent one positional shift. The relationship between the numeric positions representing a ciphertext character (c) and a plaintext character (p) can be expressed as $c=(p+5) \bmod 26$.

Listing 2.1. The plaintext-ciphertext relationship.

```
                    Alphabetic Relationship
Plaintext           ABCDEFGHIJKLMNOPQRSTUVWXYZ
Ciphertext          FGHIJKLMNOPQRSTUVWXYZABCDE


                 Numeric Relationship
Plaintext  00 01 02 03 04 05 06 07 08 09 10 11 12 13 14 15 16 17
➡18 19 20 21 22 23 24 25
Ciphertext 05 06 07 08 09 10 11 12 13 14 15 16 17 18 19 20 21 22
➡23 24 25 00 01 02 03 04
```

If each of the letters of the plaintext alphabet is sequentially assigned the numbers 0 through 25, the process of encipherment illustrated in the top portion of Listing 2.1 can be expressed as $c=(p+5)modulo\ 26$, where c represents the ciphertext character's numeric value, p represents the plaintext character's numeric value, and the *modulo 26* process requires 26 to be subtracted when the result of the addition exceeds 25.

For example, 25 MOD 26 has a value of 25, and 26 MOD 26 and 27 MOD 26 have values of 0 and 1, respectively. To verify this relationship, the lower portion of Listing 2.1 indicates the numerical relationships between the characters in the plaintext and ciphertext alphabets. This numeric relationship is based on the assignment of the values 0 through 25 to the letters in the plaintext alphabet and the shifting of the ciphertext alphabet by five positions in relation to the plaintext alphabet.

In Listing 2.1 it is obvious that the ciphertext alphabet can be shifted up to 25 positions to the right or reversed and shifted to the left. When directly shifted to the right, a series of 25 cipher alphabets can be developed because the 26th shift makes the ciphertext match the plaintext. Perhaps the most famous example of a shifted cipher alphabet is the one credited to Julius Caesar in which the original displacement between plaintext and ciphertext was three places to the right. This well-known cipher, as well as other displacement ciphers, however, is very weak because the reconstruction of plaintext may be reduced to a simple trial-and-error process. However, because you need to

start somewhere, this simple displacement process represents a good starting point for a discussion of monoalphabetic uniliteral substitution systems.

DISPLACEMENT ALPHABETS

As previously illustrated, you can develop a series of 25 direct ciphertext alphabets with respect to a plaintext alphabet when both are restricted to uppercase English letters. The top portion of Listing 2.2 contains the listing of a simple program named SHIFT.BAS, which displays all possible displaced alphabets from the standard uppercase English alphabet. In this program, the string array PLAINTXT$ is used to store each letter of the alphabet through the use of a READ statement contained in the first FOR-NEXT loop. The following pair of FOR-NEXT loops causes 25 shifted alphabets to display with respect to the original alphabet, which is displayed without any occurring shift. The bottom portion of Listing 2.2 illustrates the result obtained from the execution of SHIFT.BAS.

Listing 2.2. The SHIFT.BAS program listing.

```
REM PROGRAM SHIFT.BAS
REM This program produces a sequence of shifted alphabets
CLS
DIM PLAINTXT$(26)
FOR I = 0 TO 25
READ PLAINTXT$(I)
NEXT I
DATA "A","B","C","D","E","F","G","H","I","J","K"
DATA "L","M","N","O","P","Q","R","S","T","U","V","W","X","Y","Z"
FOR J = 0 TO 25
FOR I = 0 TO 25
PRINT PLAINTXT$((I + J) MOD 26);
NEXT I
PRINT
NEXT J

ABCDEFGHIJKLMNOPQRSTUVWXYZ
BCDEFGHIJKLMNOPQRSTUVWXYZA
```

continues

Listing 2.2. Continued

```
CDEFGHIJKLMNOPQRSTUVWXYZAB
DEFGHIJKLMNOPQRSTUVWXYZABC
EFGHIJKLMNOPQRSTUVWXYZABCD
FGHIJKLMNOPQRSTUVWXYZABCDE
GHIJKLMNOPQRSTUVWXYZABCDEF
HIJKLMNOPQRSTUVWXYZABCDEFG
IJKLMNOPQRSTUVWXYZABCDEFGH
JKLMNOPQRSTUVWXYZABCDEFGHI
KLMNOPQRSTUVWXYZABCDEFGHIJ
LMNOPQRSTUVWXYZABCDEFGHIJK
MNOPQRSTUVWXYZABCDEFGHIJKL
NOPQRSTUVWXYZABCDEFGHIJKLM
OPQRSTUVWXYZABCDEFGHIJKLMN
PQRSTUVWXYZABCDEFGHIJKLMNO
QRSTUVWXYZABCDEFGHIJKLMNOP
RSTUVWXYZABCDEFGHIJKLMNOPQ
STUVWXYZABCDEFGHIJKLMNOPQR
TUVWXYZABCDEFGHIJKLMNOPQRS
UVWXYZABCDEFGHIJKLMNOPQRST
VWXYZABCDEFGHIJKLMNOPQRSTU
WXYZABCDEFGHIJKLMNOPQRSTUV
XYZABCDEFGHIJKLMNOPQRSTUVW
YZABCDEFGHIJKLMNOPQRSTUVWX
ZABCDEFGHIJKLMNOPQRSTUVWXY
```

In addition to a direct relationship between plaintext and ciphertext alphabets, you can reverse the relationship. That is, you can reverse and displace the ciphertext alphabet with respect to the plaintext alphabet. The ciphertext can be applied to the plaintext alphabet at any one of 26 points of coincidence between the two alphabets. Thus, you can develop a series of 25 reverse ciphertext alphabets with respect to a plaintext alphabet when both are restricted to uppercase English letters. The following example illustrates a reversed ciphertext alphabet in which the first letters of both the plaintext and ciphertext alphabets coincide. Note that the reversed ciphertext alphabet can also be shifted or displaced a total of 25 times before the relationship between plaintext and ciphertext characters repeats.

Plaintext   ABCDEFGHIJKLMNOPQRSTUVWXYZ

Ciphertext   AZYXWVUTSRQPONMLKJIHGFEDCB

The relationship between a plaintext and ciphertext alphabet can be direct or reversed. For either situation, the characters in one alphabet can be shifted *n* positions, or $0<n<25$, with respect to the other alphabet prior to repetition.

You can denote the relationship between plaintext and ciphertext alphabets through the location where the ciphertext alphabet coincides with the first letter (A) of the plaintext alphabet. This location is commonly referred to as the alphabet shift key. For the ciphertext alphabet illustrated in Listing 2.1, the shift key can be expressed as $P_A=C_F$, where the uppercase *P* and *C* denote plaintext and ciphertext alphabets and the lower-case letters indicate the relationship between the two alphabets with respect to the beginning of the plaintext and ciphertext alphabets. For the reverse ciphertext alphabet illustrated in Listing 2.2, the alphabet shift key can be expressed as $P_A=R(C_A)$, where *R* indicates a reversal of the ciphertext alphabet beginning with the letter *A*.

ENCIPHERMENT

To illustrate encipherment and decipherment operations, I'll use the simple displacement relationship between ciphertext and plaintext alphabets illustrated in Listing 2.1. In that example, the alphabetic shift key, $P_A=CF$, defined the relationship between the two alphabets.

If you wish to encipher the message MEET ME IN ST LOUIS, locate M in plaintext and note that it is replaced by R in the ciphertext alphabet. In this example, each plaintext E is replaced by a ciphertext J, and so on. The plaintext message's completed encipherment yields

RJJY RJ NS XY QTZNX

In military systems, the resulting enciphered message would more than likely be rewritten for transmission into groups of five characters to minimize the effect of a transmission error and facilitate the transmission and reconstruction of the original message. Thus, if you are transmitting the message you might consider sending it as

```
RJJYR JNSXY QTZNX
```

Note that in placing the enciphered message into groups of five characters, you remove spaces between words. This is usually done to eliminate obvious word groupings. Because this message contains exactly 15 characters, it fills three groups of five characters. This is not always the case, however, and un-filled groups are normally filled with one or more predefined letters known as *message nulls*. The most common message null is the letter *X* and should not be confused with the ASCII null character that represents a blank.

Care should be taken when selecting characters to fill ending message groups and terminating messages. In many military units, messages used to be terminated with the abbreviation FTA, or one or more of those characters was used to terminate an ending message group. Not only was the abbreviation an obscene message concerning the army, but more significantly, its inclusion in an enciphered message provided an enemy intercepting the message with the ability to rapidly gain knowledge concerning a portion of the substitution process used to encipher the message. Given that insight, with some additional effort the contents of the message becomes vulnerable to decipherment.

DECIPHERMENT

Upon receipt of the enciphered message, you must know the relationship between plaintext and ciphertext to perform a decipherment operation. Although you can use the alphabet

relationship previously illustrated in Listing 2.1, that relationship is easier to use for encipherment rather than decipherment. For decipherment operations, you may wish to reverse the alphabet relationship shown in Listing 2.1—place the ciphertext alphabet at the top. Look up each letter from the enciphered message in the ciphertext alphabet and replace it with its plaintext alphabet equivalent. This produces the message MEETM EINST LOUIS, which you can rewrite to reflect the correct spacing between words.

Similar to the coding in the program SHIFT.BAS, you can easily test any enciphered message to determine if a simple monoalphabetic substitution process was used. Because only 26 plaintext-ciphertext relationships exist, you can simply displace each character in the enciphered message by a uniform amount and vary that amount 25 times to discover the contents of the plaintext. Thus, a simple monoalphabetic substitution process does not offer a significant level of protection. However, the simple monoalphabetic substitution process represents an excellent starting point for a discussion of more sophisticated substitution processes as well as the development of a series of subroutines and programs that can be used to automate encipherment and decipherment operations. In the remainder of this chapter, I'll create a series of subroutines and programs that forms the basis for coding examples constructed in the rest of this book.

AUTOMATING OPERATIONS

The process of converting plaintext to ciphertext and reversing the process can be automated to facilitate monoalphabetic operations. As explained in Chapter 1, I'll use QuickBASIC to develop the subroutines and programs presented in this chapter and the remainder of this book.

USING AN ALPHABETIC SHIFT KEY

Listing 2.3 contains the listing of the program CIPHER1.BAS, which can be used to create a ciphertext alphabet based on the

use of a defined alphabetic shift key. In this program, the string array PLAINTEXT is used to store the standard sequence of upper-case letters contained in the English alphabet; the string array CIPHERTEXT is used to store the resulting cipher alphabet shifted according to an alphabetic shift key. Note that the subroutine INITIALIZE is used to initialize the plaintext values into the array PLAINTEXT. In fact, in this and subsequent programs presented in this book, I'll use common subroutines (when possible) to facilitate the construction of specific programs or program segments developed to perform predefined operations. This will provide you with a "construction set" of routines that can be used to tailor the development of programs to their specific requirements.

Listing 2.3. The CIPHER1.BAS program listing.

```
REM PROGRAM CIPHER1.BAS
DIM PLAINTEXT$(25), CIPHERTEXT$(25)
CLS
GOSUB INITIALIZE
1       INPUT "Enter UPPERCASE Alphabetic Shift Key: ", K$
        FOR I = 0 TO 25
        IF K$ = PLAINTEXT$(I) GOTO 2
        NEXT I
        PRINT "You must enter a letter from A to Z"
        GOTO 1
2       REM Position I represents shift key letter
GOSUB FORMCIPHER
GOSUB PRTOUT
END
INITIALIZE:
        REM Initialize plaintext values
        FOR I = 0 TO 25
        READ PLAINTEXT$(I)
        NEXT I
        DATA "A","B","C","D","E","F","G","H","I","J","K","L","M","N"
        DATA "O","P","Q","R","S","T","U","V","W","X","Y","Z"
RETURN
FORMCIPHER:
        REM Routine to form CIPHERTEXT alphabet based upon defined
```

```
➥shift key
        J = I + 1
        FOR K = 0 TO 25
        CIPHERTEXT$(K) = PLAINTEXT$((K + J) MOD 26)
        NEXT K
RETURN
PRTOUT:
        REM Print results
        FOR I = 0 TO 25
        PRINT CIPHERTEXT$(I);
        NEXT I
        PRINT
RETURN
END
```

In Listing 2.3, after the PLAINTEXT array is initialized, the INPUT statement displays the message Enter UPPERCASE Alphabetic Shift Key, which is read into the string labeled K$. The value of K$ is compared against the alphabet to insure that an uppercase letter was entered. If this is not the case, an error message is displayed and the program branches back to the statement labeled 1, causing the message Enter UPPERCASE Alphabetic Shift Key to redisplay. Assuming an uppercase letter is entered, the subroutine FORMCIPHER is invoked. In this subroutine, the position in the plaintext alphabet in which the shift key character equaled a plaintext character plus one is saved by assigning I+1 to the variable J. The reason I+1 is assigned to J is because the alphabet needs to be rotated through the position of the alphabetic shift key. For example, assume C was entered as the alphabetic shift key. Its position in the array PLAINTEXT$ is 2 because the index starts at 0. To shift the alphabet so it starts at the letter D you must add 1 to the position of the shift character.

The FOR-NEXT statement in the subroutine FORMCIPHER assigns 26 characters to the array CIPHERTEXT$ by adding the index K in the loop (which varies in value from 0 to 25) to the value of J using the MOD 26 operator. Thus, when K is 0 and the shift key is C, (K+J) MOD 26 is 3, which results in D being assigned

to `CIPHERTEXT$(0)`. Similarly, when the shift key is C and K has a value of 25, `(K+J)MOD 26` has a value of 2, which results in the assignment of C to `CIPHERTEXT$(25)`.

Once the FORMCIPHER subroutine is completed, the main part of the program invokes the subroutine PRTOUT, which prints the new alphabet based on the entered alphabetic shift key.

Listing 2.4 illustrates several examples of the execution of CIPHER1.BAS. Note that the use of Z as the alphabetic shift key results in a full rotation of the alphabet.

Listing 2.4. CIPHER1.BAS execution examples.

```
Enter UPPERCASE Alphabetic Shift Key: B
CDEFGHIJKLMNOPQRSTUVWXYZAB
Enter UPPERCASE Alphabetic Shift Key: D
EFGHIJKLMNOPQRSTUVWXYZABCD
Enter UPPERCASE Alphabetic Shift Key: Q
RSTUVWXYZABCDEFGHIJKLMNOPQ
Enter UPPERCASE Alphabetic Shift Key: Z
ABCDEFGHIJKLMNOPQRSTUVWXYZ
```

CONVERTING TO CIPHERTEXT

You can build on the program CIPHER1.BAS to expand its capability so it can convert plaintext to ciphertext. Listing 2.5 contains the program listing for this new program, named CIPHER2.BAS. This elementary program enciphers a one-line message based on an alphabetic shift key.

Listing 2.5. The CIPHER2.BAS program listing.

```
REM PROGRAM CIPHER2.BAS
CLS
PRINT "This program enciphers a one-line message based on an
↪alphabetic shift key"
DIM PLAINTEXT$(26), CIPHERTEXT$(26)
GOSUB INITIALIZE
1       INPUT "Enter UPPERCASE Alphabetic Shift Key: ", K$
```

```
          FOR I = 0 TO 25
          IF K$ = PLAINTEXT$(I) GOTO 2
          NEXT I
          PRINT "You must enter a letter from A to Z"
          GOTO 1
2         REM Position I represents shift key letter
GOSUB FORMCIPHER
          PRINT "Enter your message in UPPERCASE: "
          INPUT TEXT$
          MSGLEN = LEN(TEXT$)
GOSUB MSGENCIPHER
GOSUB PRTOUT
END
INITIALIZE:
          REM Initialize plaintext values
          FOR I = 0 TO 25
          READ PLAINTEXT$(I)
          NEXT I
          DATA "A","B","C","D","E","F","G","H","I","J","K","L","M","N"
          DATA "O","P","Q","R","S","T","U","V","W","X","Y","Z"
RETURN
FORMCIPHER:
          REM Routine to form CIPHERTEXT alphabet based upon defined
➥shift key
          J = I + 1
          FOR K = 0 TO 25
          CIPHERTEXT$(K) = PLAINTEXT$((K + J) MOD 26)
          NEXT K
RETURN
MSGENCIPHER:
          REM Convert plaintext to ciphertext
          FOR I = 1 TO MSGLEN
          FOR J = 0 TO 25
          IF MID$(TEXT$, I, 1) = PLAINTEXT$(J) THEN GOTO 5
          NEXT J
5         MID$(TEXT$, I, 1) = CIPHERTEXT$(J)
          NEXT I
RETURN
```

continues

Listing 2.5. Continued

```
PRTOUT:
        REM Print results
        PRINT "Resulting enciphered message is: "
        PRINT TEXT$
RETURN
END
```

Note the new additions in Listing 2.5—specifically, the lines from PRINT "Enter your message in UPPERCASE" to END, and the sub-routine MSGENCIPHER.

The statements following the referenced PRINT statement simply accept a one-line message and store it in the string variable TEXT$, obtain the length of the message through the use of the LEN statement, store the length of the message in the variable MSGLEN, invoke the subroutine MSGENCIPHER, and output or print the results obtained from an encipherment of the message by invoking the subroutine PRTOUT. Thus, the key to encipherment once the ciphertext is developed through the use of an alphabetic shift key is the subroutine MSGENCIPHER.

THE SUBROUTINE MSGENCIPHER

The subroutine MSGENCIPHER contains a nested pair of FOR-NEXT loops in which I is varied in the outer loop from 1 to the last character of the message denoted by MSGLEN. In the inner loop, J is varied from 0 to 25 and is used to match each plaintext character in the message to its equivalent PLAINTEXT array character position through the use of the MID function. For example, when I has a value of 1, MID$(TEXT$, I, 1) extracts the first character from the string TEXT$, which, when used in the IF statement, is compared to the value of the string variable PLAINTEXT$(J). As J is varied from 0 to 25, a value is reached in which the extracted character from TEXT$ equals a character in the PLAINTEXT$ string array and a branch to the statement label 5 occurs. At that location, the character in the string TEXT$ is replaced by the character in the CIPHERTEXT$ array located at position J. Thus,

each character in the plaintext message is replaced by a character from the shifted alphabet whose position coincides with the unshifted alphabet plaintext character.

Listing 2.6 illustrates the execution of the program CIPHER2.BAS using B as the alphabetic shift key to form the cipher alphabet. Note that at this point you have to eliminate spaces between words because there is no space character in this plaintext or ciphertext alphabet. Later in this book I'll develop a routine that removes spaces between words, enabling a user to enter a plaintext message in a more natural manner.

Listing 2.6. A CIPHER2.BAS execution example.

```
This program enciphers a one-line message based on an alphabetic
➥shift key
Enter UPPERCASE Alphabetic Shift Key: B
Enter your message in UPPERCASE
? BIDFIVEPOINTTWOMILLION
Resulting enciphered message is:
DKFHKXGRQKPVVYQOKNNKQP
```

LIMITING THE EFFECT OF ERRORS

The meaning of an enciphered message can be adversely affected by a human typing error or a transmission or transcription error. In these situations, a mistake that adds or omits a character jumbles the decipherment and the meaning of a message. A mechanism is needed to limit the effect of errors caused by humans or technology. One common mechanism has its roots dating to the development of military systems and is known as character grouping—the most common method is the placement of enciphered text into groups of five characters for transmission.

To place ciphertext into groups of five characters, I'll modify the CIPHER2.BAS program with the inclusion of a new subroutine. This subroutine, appropriately named GROUPBY5, replaces the subroutine PRTOUT contained in the CIPHER2.BAS program.

THE SUBROUTINE GROUPBY5

Listing 2.7 contains the contents of the subroutine GROUPBY5. That subroutine uses the variable L as a group counter. When invoked, the subroutine sets the value of L to 1. The FOR-NEXT loop in the subroutine prints one character at a time using the MID$ function, which extracts a character from the string variable TEXT$. After a character is printed, the value of the FOR-NEXT loop index (I) divided by five is compared to the value of L. If the value of I/5 equals the value of L, five characters are printed and a branch to the label 6 occurs. At that label, the PRINT statement generates a space. If the value of I/5 does not equal the value of L, a branch to the label 7 occurs and the FOR-NEXT loop terminates the current index value of the loop.

Listing 2.7. The subroutine GROUPBY5 listing.

```
GROUPBY5:
        L = 1
        FOR I = 1 TO MSGLEN
        PRINT MID$(TEXT$, I, 1)
        IF I / 5 = L THEN GOTO 6
        GOTO 7
6       PRINT " ";
        L = L + 1
7       NEXT I
RETURN
```

One of the more famous messages transmitted using group-ings of five characters was sent by Takeo Yoshikawa, a Japa-nese naval ensign assigned as a consultate secretary to the Japanese consultate in Honolulu. At 6 p.m. on December 6, 1941, he sent his final message using what was known as Oite to the Japanese and PA-K2 to American code breakers. This message contained 44 groups of five characters and was trans-mitted to Tokyo via RCA communications at a cost of $6.82.

The message transmitted by Ensign Yoshikawa reported the arrival of an American battleship and a mine sweeper into port and provided a summary of the number of ships at anchor and ships in dock in Honolulu by category—battleships, light cruisers, destroyers, and mine sweepers. The message also noted that it appeared that no air reconnaissance was being conducted by the U.S. fleet's air arm.

Although American cryptanalysts were able to crack messages transmitted in a PA-K2 code, doing so required an average of three days. Unfortunately, the contents of this message were deciphered well after the attack on Pearl Harbor began.

PROGRAM CIPHER3.BAS

Listing 2.8 contains the listing of the main body of the program CIPHER3.BAS. That program includes the subroutine GROUPBY5, which groups a line of enciphered text into groups of five characters. Listing 2.9 illustrates an example of the execution of the CIPHER3.BAS program using the alphabetic shift key B and shows the five-character grouping of the enciphered message. If you are familiar with military systems, you may wonder why the GROUPBY5 subroutine leaves the last group with less than five characters instead of filling the group by adding Xs or some similar group terminator character. The reason for not doing so at this time is because this program operates only on one message line at a time. Thus, before you terminate an unfilled group, you should first modify your program to read and process multiple lines of plaintext.

Listing 2.8. The program listing of the main portion of CIPHER3.BAS.

```
REM PROGRAM CIPHER3.BAS
DIM PLAINTEXT$(25), CIPHERTEXT$(25)
CLS
        GOSUB INITIALIZE
```

continues

Listing 2.8. Continued

```
1       INPUT "Enter UPPERCASE Alphabetic Shift Key: ", K$
        FOR I = 0 TO 25
        IF K$ = PLAINTEXT$(I) GOTO 2
        NEXT I
        PRINT "You must enter a letter from A to Z"
        GOTO 1
2       REM Position I represents shift key letter
GOSUB FORMCIPHER
        PRINT "Enter your message in UPPERCASE: "
        INPUT TEXT$
        MSGLEN = LEN(TEXT$)
GOSUB MSGENCIPHER
        REM Print results
        PRINT "Resulting enciphered message is: "
GOSUB GROUPBY5
        END
```

Listing 2.9. A sample execution of the program CIPHER3.BAS.

```
Enter UPPERCASE Alphabetic Shift Key: B
Enter your message in UPPERCASE:
? BUYFIVETHOUSANDSHARESOFGAMMAINDUSTRIES
Resulting enciphered message is:
DWAHK XGVJQ WUCPF UJCTG UQHIC OOCKP FWUVT KGU
```

PROCESSING MULTIPLE-LINE MESSAGES

Because I want to have the ability to read a message containing multiple lines of text, I'll modify the previously constructed program with the addition of several subroutines. One subroutine I'll develop will permit a message to be input from the keyboard or a previously created file. To provide users with the capability to enter text more naturally, this subroutine will also permit the user to enter words with spaces between words because the program will be responsible for their removal. Other subroutines will convert the plaintext message into ciphertext, position the enciphered text into groups of five

characters for printing, and terminate the last group of characters with an appropriate number of Xs to fill any terminating group that has less than five characters.

THE SUBROUTINE MSGFILE

Listing 2.10 contains the contents of the subroutine labeled MSGFILE. This subroutine performs three major functions. First, it permits the user to assign filenames for the file used to store a plaintext and the resulting ciphertext message, or to select the default filenames MESSAGE.DAT for storing the plaintext message and CIPHERTX.DAT for storing the enciphered message. The second function performed by MSGFILE is to remove spaces between words. The third function performed by this subroutine stores the resulting plaintext message in which any spaces between words were removed.

Listing 2.10. The subroutine MSGFILE.

```
MSGFILE:
        REM Routine to assign I/O files and accept keyboard or file
➡input
        REM and remove spaces between words
                INPUT "Enter filename to store plaintext message,
                    default=MESSAGE.DAT", INFILE$
                IF INFILE$ = "" THEN INFILE$ = "MESSAGE.DAT"
                INPUT "Enter filename to store enciphered message,
                    default=CIPHERTX.DAT
                IF OUTFILE$ = "" THEN OUTFILE$ = "CIPHERTX.DAT"
                INPUT  "Select keyboard (k) or file (f)
                    message input: ", IN$
                IF IN$ = "F" OR IN$ = "f" THEN RETURN
                OPEN INFILE$ FOR OUTPUT AS #1
            REM Routine to place enciphered message on a file removing
                spaces between words
                    PRINT "Enter you message - place a / at the
➡beginning of each line"
                        PRINT "that should remain in plaintext and a \ on a
                            separate line"
```

continues

Listing 2.10. Continued

```
                    PRINT "to indicate the end of the enciphered
➡message"
AGN:                LINE INPUT TEXT$
                    IF MID$(TEXT$, 1, 1) = "/" THEN GOTO XT
                    NTEXT$ = ""
                    FOR I = 1 TO LEN(TEXT$)
                    NTEXT$ = NTEXT$ + LTRIM$(MID$(TEXT$, I, 1))
                    NEXT I
                    WRITE #1, NTEXT$
                    IF MID$(TEXT$, 1, 1) = "\" GOTO DONE
                    GOTO AGN
XT:                 WRITE #1, TEXT$
                    GOTO AGN
DONE:                  CLOSE 31
RETURN
```

The first portion of the subroutine MSGFILE prompts the user to enter filenames for storing a plaintext message and its resulting enciphered message. If the user simply presses Return, the default filenames MESSAGE.DAT and CIPHERTX.DAT are used. Otherwise, the subroutine prompts the user to enter the appropriate plaintext and ciphertext filenames.

The second major routine in MSGFILE performs the actual placement of keyboard-entered plaintext on a file and removes spaces between words. To facilitate the transmission of enciphered messages, this portion of the subroutine permits users to prefix each heading message line with a slash (/) character if they do not want that message line to be enciphered. This allows a header portion of a message to be ignored during the encipherment process. The transmission of the enciphered text with a cleartext header facilitates its distribution to the appropriate recipient. To indicate the end of the message, a backslash (\) character must be entered by itself on a separate line.

The FOR-NEXT loop in the second half of the subroutine MSGFILE uses the LTRIM$ statement to remove spaces between

words. This FOR-NEXT loop is invoked only when the beginning of a line does not contain a slash character. Because LTRIM$ removes leading spaces in a string, its use in the FOR-NEXT loop places a line of plaintext in which all spaces have been removed into the string variable NTEXT$.

THE SUBROUTINE CONVERTSTORE

The following subroutine reads the contents of previously stored messages one line at a time, converts each message into its enciphered text, and stores the enciphered text on a line-by-line basis in the file whose name is assigned to the string variable OUTFILE$. Listing 2.11 contains the statements in the subroutine CONVERTSTORE, which performs the previously mentioned functions.

Listing 2.11. The subroutine CONVERTSTORE.

```
CONVERTSTORE:
        REM Routine to convert and store ciphertext on a file
        OPEN INFILE$ FOR INPUT AS #1
        OPEN OUTFILE$ FOR OUTPUT AS #2
        DO UNTIL EOF(1)
                INPUT #1, TEXT$
                MSGLEN = LEN(TEXT$)
                IF MID$(TEXT$, 1, 1) = "/" THEN GOTO CLEARTXT
                IF MID$(TEXT$, 1, 1) = "\" THEN GOTO DONE1
                REM Convert plaintext to ciphertext
                        FOR I = 1 TO MSGLEN
                        FOR J = 0 TO 25
                        IF MID$(TEXT$, I, 1) = PLAINTEXT$(J)
➡THEN GOTO GOTIT
                        NEXT J
GOTIT:                  MID#(TEXT$, I, 1) = CIPHERTEXT$(J)
                        NEXT I
CLEARTXT:               WRITE #2, TEXT$
        LOOP
DONE1:          CLOSE #2
        RETURN
```

After opening the file whose name was assigned to the string variable INFILE$ for input and the file whose name was assigned to OUTFILE$ for output, the subroutine uses a DO UNTIL loop to read each message line from the file containing the plaintext message. Within the DO UNTIL loop, each line is processed based on the first character in the line.

If the first character in a line is a slash, a branch to the label CLEARTXT occurs and the conversion of plaintext to enciphered text is bypassed. If the first character in a line is a backslash, the end of the previously stored message has been reached and a branch to the label DONE1 occurs. This terminates the loop, closes the previously opened file #2, and causes an exit from the subroutine to occur.

If the first character in each line is neither a slash nor a backslash character, the subroutine converts each plaintext character in the line into its equivalent ciphertext character. This is accomplished through the use of a pair of nested FOR-NEXT loops. The outer loop cycles through each of the characters in a line retrieved from the file containing the plaintext. The inner loop compares (on a character-by-character basis) the plaintext character to each character in the string array PLAINTEXT$. When a match occurs, a branch to the label GOTIT occurs. At that label, the plaintext character is replaced by the ciphertext character whose position in the array CIPHERTEXT$ is the same as the position of the plaintext character in the array PLAINTEXT$.

THE SUBROUTINE PRTOUT

Now that I have developed subroutines to place a message on a file and process and convert the message to enciphered text that is stored on another file, I am ready to print the results. To do this I will develop a subroutine named PRTOUT that will process the file containing the enciphered text so that no more than 25 characters (or five groups of five characters) are displayed on a line. I have limited the printout of enciphered text to 25 characters per line to facilitate manual operations for users

that wish to use the resulting display of the enciphered message in place of the file containing the enciphered text.

Listing 2.12 contains the contents of the subroutine PRTOUT. After using an INPUT statement to display the message informing a user to press Return, the subroutine clears the display and sets the string variable TEMP$ to a null value. The message "Resulting enciphered message is:" is then displayed and the file assigned to the variable OUTFILE$ is opened for input. Note that the enciphered text was previously stored on the file assigned to the variable OUTFILE$; thus, this subroutine processes the enciphered message.

Listing 2.12. The subroutine PRTOUT.

```
PRTOUT: REM Subroutine to print results
        INPUT "Press Return key to display resulting enciphered
➥message", p$
        CLS : TEMP$ = ""
        PRINT "Resulting enciphered message is:"
        OPEN OUTFILE$ FOR INPUT AS #2
        DO UNTIL EOF(2)
                INPUT #2, TEXT$
                IF MID$(TEXT$, 1, 1) = "/" THEN PRINT
➥RIGHT$(TEXT$,
                    LEN(TEXT$) - 1)
                IF MID$(TEXT$, 1, 1) = "/" THEN GOTO NOGROUP
                IF TEMP$ = "" GOTO BLANK          'blank string
                IF TEMP$ = TEMP$ + TEXT$          'concatenate
                TEXT$ = TEMP$
                TEMP$ = ""
BLANK:          MSGLEN = LEN(TEXT$)
                IF MSGLEN >= 25 THEN GOTO BIG
                TEMP$ = TEXT4
                GOTO NOGROUP                      'less than 25
                                                 ➥characters
BIG:            FOR I = 26 TO MSGLEN              'place remainder
                                                 ➥of string
                                                     into temp
```

continues

Listing 2.12. Continued

```
                    TEMP$ = TEMP$ + MID$(TEXT$, I, 1)
                    NEXT I
                    MSGLEN = 25
                    GOSUB GROUPBY5:                      'print 25
                                                      ➥characters
          NOGROUP: LOOP
                    TEXT$ = TEMP$
                    MSGLEN = LEN(TEXT$)
                    IF MSGLEN <= 25 THEN GOSUB GROUPBY5
                    IF MSGLEN <= 25 THEN RETURN         'done printing
               WHILE MSGLEN > 25
                    TEMP$ = LEFT$(TEXT$, 25)            'get first 25
                                                      ➥characters
                                                          in string

                    TEMPR$ = RIGHT$(TEXT$, MSGLEN - 25)
                    TEXT$ = TEMP$
                    MSGLEN = LEN(TEXT$)
                    GOSUB GROUPBY5
                    TEXT$ = TEMPR$
                    MSGLEN = LEN(TEXT$)
               WEND
                    TEXT$ = TEMPR$
                    MSGLEN = LEN(TEXT$)
                    GOSUB GROUPBY5
          RETURN
```

The DO UNTIL loop processes the lines on the enciphered file. Each line is read into the string variable TEXT$. The first two IF statements check for the presence of a slash. If a slash occurs in the first character position in a line, the first IF statement causes the line to print without the slash. Because a slash indicates the line should be treated as cleartext, the second IF statement simply skips the remaining statements in the loop by branching to the label NOGROUP.

The first time PRTOUT is invoked, the string TEMP$ is set to the null string. Thus, the first time through the DO UNTIL loop, the

third IF statement causes a branch to the label BLANK to occur. At that label the length of the retrieved line of ciphertext is determined through the use of the LEN function. If the length of the line equals or exceeds 25 characters, a branch to the label BIG occurs. If the length of the line does not exceed 25 characters, there are not enough characters to print 25 characters on one line. At this point, the characters assigned to the variable TEXT$ are assigned to the variable TEMP$ and a branch to the label NOGROUP occurs to terminate one cycle through the loop.

When the value of TEMP$ is not a null string, the contents of the next line of ciphertext are concatenated or joined to the contents of TEMP$. The contents of TEMP$ are then assigned to TEXT$, and TEMP$ is reset to a null string. In this manner you can continue to cycle through the contents of the enciphered file until you either reach the end of the file or the length of the variable TEXT$ equals or exceeds 25 characters.

When the length of TEXT$ equals or exceeds 25 characters, a branch to the label BIG occurs. At that location, the FOR-NEXT loop places the remainder of the contents of TEXT$ that exceed 25 characters into the variable TEMP$. The message length variable MSGLEN is then set to 25 and the subroutine GROUPBY5 is called. That subroutine (discussed in more detail in the next section in this chapter) actually prints the characters in groups of fives and assigns Xs to fill the last group if that group contains less than five characters.

When all lines in the file assigned to OUTFILE$ are read, exit the DO UNTIL loop. At this point, you need to print the remaining enciphered text stored in the variable TEMP$. To do this, assign the contents of TEMP$ to TEXT$ and obtain its length. If the length of TEXT$ is less than or equal to 25 characters, invoke the subroutine GROUPBY5 to print the last 25 (or less) characters in the enciphered message and exit the subroutine. If there are more than 25 characters in TEXT$, use a WHILE-WEND loop to print the contents of TEXT$. Assign the first 25 characters in TEXT$ to TEMP$ using the LEFT$ function. The remaining characters in the string

TEXT$ are then assigned to the variable TEMPR$. After the contents of TEMP$ are assigned to TEXT$, the message length is determined and the subroutine GROUPBY5 is invoked. The contents of TEMPR$ are then assigned to TEXT$, the length of TEXT$ is determined, and the subroutine GROUPBY5 is again invoked, this time printing the remaining portion of characters that exceeded 25 in length. When less than 25 characters remain in TEMPR$, the WHILE-WEND loop terminates. At that point the contents of TEMPR$ are assigned to TEXT$, its length is determined, and the subroutine GROUPBY5 is invoked for the last time.

MODIFYING SUBROUTINE GROUPBY5

As previously constructed, this subroutine performs the actual printing of characters in groups of five. You can modify this subroutine so that it fills the last group with Xs (if there are less than five characters in the group). Listing 2.13 contains the statement in this modified subroutine.

Listing 2.13. The subroutine GROUPBY5.

```
GROUPBY5:
        L = 1
        FOR I = 1 TO MSGLEN
                PRINT MID$(TEXT$, I, 1);
                IF I / 5 = L THEN GOTO AGROUP
                GOTO NGROUP
AGROUP:         PRINT " ";
                L = L + 1
NGROUP: NEXT I
        NUMX = 5 - MSGLEN MOD 5
        IF NUMX = 5 OR NUMX = 0 THEN GOTO PRTBLK
        FOR I = 1 TO NUMX
        PRINT "X";
        NEXT I
PRTBLK: PRINT
RETURN
```

When the subroutine is invoked, the variable L is set to 1 and the FOR-NEXT loop cycles through the contents of the string

variable TEXT$, printing one character at a time. If the index I of the FOR-NEXT loop divided by 5 equals L, five characters print and a branch to the label AGROUP occurs. At that location, the PRINT statement prints a space, providing a space between groups of five characters. The variable L is then incremented and the loop ends. If a group of five characters is not printed, a branch to the label NGROUP occurs, bypassing the printing of the space.

Once the FOR-NEXT loop is completed, you must determine if a group did not have five characters, a condition that can only occur when the last line in the enciphered message is processed. Here, the value of the variable NUMX determines the number of Xs that must be added to fill the last group. Invoke the next FOR-NEXT loop to print the terminating Xs only if NUMX is greater than 0 or less than 5. Otherwise, a branch to the label PRTBLK occurs, which terminates a previous PRINT statement ending with a semicolon so that the next cycle through the subroutine GROUPBY5 has succeeding groups placed on a new line.

PROGRAM CIPHER4.BAS

Examine the following listing (Listing 2.14) of the complete program that includes the previously mentioned subroutines. This program is contained in the file CIPHER4.BAS on the convenience disk. You should note that the main portion of CIPHER4.BAS closely resembles CIPHER3.BAS. Calls using the GOSUB statement, however, were added to access the subroutines MSGFILE, CONVERTSTORE, and PRTOUT (PRTOUT accesses the subroutine GROUPBY5). You should also note the inclusion of several PRINT statements at the beginning of the program to better describe its operation.

Listing 2.14. The CIPHER4.BAS program listing.

```
REM PROGRAM CIPHER4.BAS
DIM PLAINTEXT$(26), CIPHERTEXT$(26)
CLS
        GOSUB INITIALIZE
```

continues

Listing 2.14. Continued

```
        PRINT "CIPHER4.BAS PROGRAM accepts spaces between words
➥in a plaintext "
        PRINT "message and selectively enciphers the message
➥using a simple"
        PRINT "monoalphabetic substitution process."
        PRINT
1       INPUT "Enter UPPERCASE Alphabetic Shift Key: ", K$
        FOR I = 0 TO 25
        IF K$ = PLAINTEXT$(I) GOTO 2
        NEXT I
        PRINT "You must enter a letter from A to Z"
        GOTO 1
2       REM Position I represents shift key letter
GOSUB FORMCIPHER              'create cipher alphabet
GOSUB MSGFILE                 'assign I/O files, place message on a
                             ➥file
GOSUB CONVERTSTORE            'convert and store ciphertext on a
                             ➥file
GOSUB PRTOUT                  'print results
END
INITIALIZE:
        REM Initialize plaintext values
        FOR I = 0 TO 25
        READ PLAINTEXT$(I)
        NEXT I
        DATA "A","B","C","D","E","F","G","H","I","J","K","L","M","N"
        DATA "O","P","Q","R","S","T","U","V","W","X","Y","Z"
RETURN
FORMCIPHER:
        REM Routine to form CIPHERTEXT alphabet based upon defined
➥shift key
        J = I + 1
        FOR K = 0 TO 25
        CIPHERTEXT$(K) = PLAINTEXT$((K + J) MOD 26)
        NEXT K
RETURN
MSGFILE:
        REM Routine to assign I/O files and accept keyboard or file
➥input
```

```
          REM and remove spaces between words
                  INPUT "Enter filename to store plaintext message,
➥(default=MESSAGE.DAT):",
                  IF INFILE$ = "" THEN INFILE$ = "MESSAGE.DAT"
                  INPUT "Enter filename to store enciphered message,
➥(default=CIPHER.DAT):",
                  IF OUTFILE$ = "" THEN OUTFILE$ = "CIPHER.DAT"
                  INPUT "Select keyboard (k) or file (f) message
➥input: ", IN$
                  IF IN$ = "F" OR IN$ = "f" THEN RETURN
                  OPEN INFILE$ FOR OUTPUT AS #1
          REM Routine to place message on a file removing spaces
➥between words
                  PRINT "Enter your message - place a / at the
➥beginning of each line"
                  PRINT "that should remain in plaintext and a \ on a
➥separate line"
                  PRINT "to indicate the end of the enciphered
➥message"
                  PRINT
AGN:              LINE INPUT TEXT$
                  IF MID$(TEXT$, 1, 1) = "/" THEN GOTO XT
                  NTEXT$ = ""
                  FOR I = 1 TO LEN(TEXT$)
                  NTEXT$ = NTEXT$ + LTRIM$(MID$(TEXT$, I, 1))
                  NEXT I
                  WRITE #1, NTEXT$
                  IF MID$(TEXT$, 1, 1) = "\" GOTO DONE
                  GOTO AGN
XT:               WRITE #1, TEXT$
                  GOTO AGN
DONE:               CLOSE #1
RETURN
CONVERTSTORE:
          REM Routine to convert and store ciphertext on a file
          OPEN INFILE$ FOR INPUT AS #1
          OPEN OUTFILE$ FOR OUTPUT AS #2
```

continues

Listing 2.14. Continued

```
                DO UNTIL EOF(1)
                        INPUT #1, TEXT$
                        MSGLEN = LEN(TEXT$)
                        IF MID$(TEXT$, 1, 1) = "/" THEN GOTO CLEARTXT
                        IF MID$(TEXT$, 1, 1) = "\" THEN GOTO DONE1
                        REM Convert plaintext to ciphertext
                                FOR I = 1 TO MSGLEN
                                FOR J = 0 TO 25
                                IF MID$(TEXT$, I, 1) = PLAINTEXT$(J)
➥THEN GOTO GOTIT
                                NEXT J
GOTIT:                          MID$(TEXT$, I, 1) = CIPHERTEXT$(J)
                                NEXT I
CLEARTXT:               WRITE #2, TEXT$
        LOOP
DONE1:          CLOSE #2
RETURN
PRTOUT: REM Subroutine to print results
        INPUT "Press Return key to display resulting enciphered
➥message ", p$
        CLS : TEMP$ = ""
        PRINT "Resulting enciphered message is:"
        OPEN OUTFILE$ FOR INPUT AS #2
        DO UNTIL EOF(2)
                INPUT #2, TEXT$
                IF MID$(TEXT$, 1, 1) = "/" THEN PRINT
➥RIGHT$(TEXT$, LEN(TEXT$) - 1)
                IF MID$(TEXT$, 1, 1) = "/" THEN GOTO NOGROUP
                IF TEMP$ = "" GOTO BLANK            'blank string
                TEMP$ = TEMP$ + TEXT$               'concatenate
                TEXT$ = TEMP$
                TEMP$ = ""
BLANK:          MSGLEN = LEN(TEXT$)
                IF MSGLEN >= 25 THEN GOTO BIG
                TEMP$ = TEXT$
                GOTO NOGROUP                        'less than 25
                                                  ➥characters
```

```
BIG:              FOR I = 26 TO MSGLEN              'place remainder
                                                   ➥of string into temp
                  TEMP$ = TEMP$ + MID$(TEXT$, I, 1)
                  NEXT I
                  MSGLEN = 25
                  GOSUB GROUPBY5:                   'print 25
                                                   ➥characters
NOGROUP: LOOP
                  TEXT$ = TEMP$                     'print remainder
                  MSGLEN = LEN(TEXT$)
                  IF MSGLEN <= 25 THEN GOSUB GROUPBY5
                  IF MSGLEN <= 25 THEN RETURN       'done printing
            WHILE MSGLEN > 25
                  TEMP$ = LEFT$(TEXT$, 25)          'get first 25
                                                   ➥characters in string
                  TEMPR$ = RIGHT$(TEXT$, MSGLEN - 25)
                  TEXT$ = TEMP$
                  MSGLEN = LEN(TEXT$)
                  GOSUB GROUPBY5
                  TEXT$ = TEMPR$
                  MSGLEN = LEN(TEXT$)
            WEND
                  TEXT$ = TEMPR$
                  MSGLEN = LEN(TEXT$)
                  GOSUB GROUPBY5
RETURN
GROUPBY5:
        L = 1
        FOR I = 1 TO MSGLEN
                  PRINT MID$(TEXT$, I, 1);
                  IF I / 5 = L THEN GOTO AGROUP
                  GOTO NGROUP
AGROUP:           PRINT " ";
                  L = L + 1
NGROUP: NEXT I
        NUMX = 5 - MSGLEN MOD 5
        IF NUMX = 5 OR NUMX = 0 THEN GOTO PRTBLK
        FOR I = 1 TO NUMX
```

continues

Listing 2.14. Continued

```
        PRINT "X";
        NEXT I
PRTBLK: PRINT
RETURN
END
```

PROGRAM EXECUTION

To illustrate the use of CIPHER4.BAS, execute the program just developed. The top portion of Listing 2.15 illustrates the execution of the program, which displays program information and enables the user to enter a message. In this example the first two lines of the message were entered with the slash as a prefix character to ensure that those lines remained in cleartext. After the two-line heading, the next four lines required encipherment and were entered without a slash character used as a prefix. Finally, the backslash character was entered on a separate line to indicate the termination of the message.

Listing 2.15. The execution of CIPHER4.BAS.

```
CIPHER4.BAS PROGRAM accepts spaces between words in a plaintext
message and selectively enciphers the message using a simple
monoalphabetic substitution process.
Enter UPPERCASE Alphabetic Shift Key: B
Enter filename to store plaintext message, default=MESSAGE.DAT
Enter filename to store enciphered message, default=CIPHERTX.DAT
Select keyboard (k) or file (f) message input: K
Enter your message - place a / at the beginning of each line
that should remain in plaintext and a \ on a separate line
to indicate the end of the enciphered message

/TO ALL BRANCH CHIEFS
/FROM PRESIDENT V.F. SMALL
DUE TO THE PRESENT STATE OF THE ECONOMY WE MUST TERMINATE
TWENTY PERCENT OF OUR EMPLOYEES BY NEXT FRIDAY STOP
YOU MUST PREPARE YOUR HIT LIST THIS WEEKEND AND TRANSMIT
```

```
THAT LIST IN ENCIPHERED FORM TO ME BY NINE AM MONDAY STOP
\
Press Return key to display resulting enciphered message




Resulting enciphered message is:
TO ALL BRANCH CHIEFS
FROM PRESIDENT V.F. SMALL
FWGVQ VJGRT GUGPV UVCVG QHVJG
GEQPQ OAYGO WUVVG TOKPC VGVYG
PVARG TEGPV QHQWT GORNQ AGGUD
APGZV HTKFC AUVQR AQWOW UVRTG
RCTGA QWTJK VNKUV VJKUY GGMGP
FCPFV TCPUO KVVJC VNKUV KPGPE
KRJGT GFHQT OVQOG DAPKP GCOOQ
PFCAU VQRXX
```

The lower portion of Listing 2.15 illustrates the resulting enciphered message printed in groups of five characters. Note that the first two lines of heading information are simply printed without alteration; the body of the message is both enciphered and printed in groups of five characters. Also note that the last group contains three characters and requires the addition of two Xs to complete the group of five. You can easily confirm this visually by noting that the message ended with the word STOP. Because a simple alphabetic shift was used for enciphering using the character B as the shift key, each character of plaintext is shifted up two positions in the alphabet. Thus, STOP becomes UVQR. Because VQR are the last three characters in the message, two Xs were added to complete the group.

PROGRAM DEFAULT FILES

To understand the contents of the default files created by CIPHER4.BAS, examine their contents after the program is executed. Listing 2.16 contains the contents of MESSAGE.DAT and CIPHERTX.DAT based upon the message (illustrated in

Listing 2.15) entered when CIPHER4.BAS was executed. As indicated in Listing 2.15, the heading is placed on a file as is, and the body of the message is placed on each file with the spaces between words removed.

Listing 2.16. The CIPHER4.BAS file contents.

```
C>TYPE MESSAGE.DAT
"/TO ALL BRANCH CHIEFS"
"/FROM PRESIDENT V.F. SMALL"
"DUETOTHEPRESENTSTATEOFTHEECONOMYWEMUSTTERMINATE"
"TWENTYPERCENTOFOUREMPLOYEESBYNEXTFRIDAYSTOP"
"YOUMUSTPREPAREYOURHITLISTTHISWEEKENDANDTRANSMIT"
"THATLISTINENCIPHEREDFORMTOMEBYNINEAMMONDAYSTOP"
"\"

C>TYPE CIPHERTX.DAT
"/TO ALL BRANCH CHIEFS"
"/FROM PRESIDENT V.F. SMALL"
"FWGVQVJGRTGUGPVUVCVGQHVJGGEQPQOAYGOWUVVGTOKPCVG"
"VYGPVARGTEGPVQHQWTGORNQAGGUDAPGZVHTKFCAUVQR"
"AQWOWUVRTGRCTGAQWTJKVNKUVVJKUYGGMGPFCPFVTCPUOKV"
"VJCVNKUVKPGPEKRJGTGFHQTOVQOGDAPKPGCOOQPFCAUVQR"

C>
```

Although simple monoalphabetic substitution produces ciphertext that offers little message protection, it provides you with a foundation for creating a program with many subroutines. Prior to moving on to more sophisticated methods of encipherment, I'll conclude this chapter by automating the decipherment process. Although you could create several new subroutines and incorporate them into your encipherment program through appropriate logic to form one program that both enciphers and deciphers messages, it may be more useful to illustrate the decipherment process by creating a separate program. That program should be named DCIPHER4.BAS to correspond to CIPHER4.BAS because they both use the simple monoalphabetic substitution process to encipher and decipher messages.

PROGRAM DCIPHER4.BAS

The process of deciphering a message is the inverse of the encipherment process. For a simple monoalphabetic substitution process, initialize the plaintext and ciphertext alphabets using the previously developed INITIALIZE and FORMCIPHER subroutines. Once the two alphabets are constructed, use a new subroutine to decipher the ciphertext characters by comparing each ciphertext character in the message to the ciphertext alphabet. When a match occurs, use the position of the character in the ciphertext alphabet as a pointer to extract a corresponding character from the plaintext alphabet. In addition to creating this new subroutine (DECIPHER), you must modify the previously created MSGFILE and PRTOUT subroutines. As you will recall, MSGFILE is used to assign I/O files and accept keyboard or file input, and PRTOUT is used to print the enciphered message. To reflect the new functions performed by those subroutines, change their names to DMSGFILE and DPRTOUT, respectively.

THE SUBROUTINE DMSGFILE

Listing 2.17 contains the statements contained in the subroutine DMSGFILE, which assigns I/O files and accepts the entry of an enciphered message from either the keyboard or from a file. Because enciphered text is grouped into five-character groups with spaces between groups, the DMSGFILE subroutine is similar to the MSGFILE subroutine because it removes spaces between groups (MSGFILE removes spaces between words). Also note that the variable INFILE$ is used to store the name of the file containing the enciphered message, and the variable OUTFILE$ is used to store the resulting plaintext deciphered message. DMSGFILE assigns files opposite to the manner in which I/O files are assigned by the subroutine MSGFILE.

Listing 2.17. The subroutine DMSGFILE.

```
DMSGFILE:
        REM Routine to assign I/O files and accept keyboard of
➥file input
      REM and remove spaces between words
            INPUT "Enter filename to store enciphered message,
                default=CIPHERTX.DAT", INFILE$
            IF INFILE$ = "" THEN INFILE$ = "CIPHERTX.DAT"
            INPUT "Enter filename to store deciphered message,
                default=MESSAGE>DAT", OUTFILE$
            IF OUTFILE$ = "" THEN OUTFILE$ = "MESSAGE.DAT"
            INPUT  "Select keyboard (k) or file (f) ciphertext
                message input: ", IN$
            IF IN$ = "F" OR IN$ = "f" THEN RETURN
            OPEN INFILE$ FOR OUTPUT AS #1
        REM Routine to place enciphered message on a file removing
        REM spaces between groups
            PRINT "Enter you message - place a / at the
➥beginning of ";
            PRINT each line"
            PRINT "that should remain in plaintext and a \
➥on a ";
            PRINT separate line"
            PRINT "to indicate the end of the enciphered
➥message"
            PRINT
AGN:        LINE INPUT TEXT$
            IF MID$(TEXT$, 1, 1) = "/" THEN GOTO XT
            NTEXT$ = ""
            FOR I = 1 TO LEN(TEXT$)
            NTEXT$ = NTEXT$ + LTRIM$(MID$(TEXT$, I, 1))
            NEXT I
            WRITE #1, NTEXT$
            IF MID$(TEXT$, 1, 1) = "\" GOTO DONE
            GOTO AGN
XT:         WRITE #1, TEXT$
            GOTO AGN
DONE:       CLOSE #1
RETURN
```

Similar to the manner in which MSGFILE was created, DMSGFILE uses the slash and backslash characters to indicate to the program that it should bypass conversion (/) or that the end of the message is reached (\). Thus, the second part of DMSGFILE, with the exception of the wording in PRINT statements, functions in the same manner as the subroutine MSGFILE used in the CIPHER4.BAS program.

THE SUBROUTINE DECIPHER

The actual deciphering process is performed by the subroutine DECIPHER (see Listing 2.18). When you examine the statements in the subroutine DECIPHER, you should note its close resemblance to the subroutine CONVERTSTORE in the CIPHER4.BAS program. The only difference between the two subroutines is the search mechanisms bounded by the nested FOR-NEXT loops. In the DECIPHER subroutine, each character in the enciphered message is compared against the ciphertext alphabet. When a match occurs, the position of the character in the ciphertext alphabet is used as a pointer to extract a character from the plaintext alphabet. You should also note that the first character of each line of data retrieved from the ciphertext file is examined to determine if a slash or backslash character is in the first position of the line. Similar to the encipherment process, the decipherment process uses those characters to bypass the decipherment process (/) or to terminate the decipherment process (\).

Listing 2.18. The subroutine DECIPHER.

```
DECIPHER:
        REM Routine to decipher and store plaintext on a file
        OPEN INFILE$ FOR INPUT AS #1
        OPEN OUTFILE$ FOR OUTPUT AS #2
        DO UNTIL EOF(1)
                INPUT #1, TEXT$
                MSGLEN = LEN(TEXT$)
                IF MID$(TEXT$, 1, 1) = "/" THEN GOTO CLEARTXT
                IF MID$(TEXT$, 1, 1) = "\" THEN GOTO DONE1
```

continues

Listing 2.18. Continued

```
                        REM Convert ciphertext to plaintext
                        FOR I = 1 TO MSGLEN
                        FOR J = 0 TO 25
                        IF MID$(TEXT$, I, 1) = CIPHERTEXT$(J)
➥THEN GOTO GOTIT
                        NEXT J
GOTIT:                  MID$(TEXT$, I, 1) = PLAINTEXT$(J)
                        NEXT I
CLEARTXT:               WRITE #2, TEXT$
            LOOP
DONE1:          CLOSE #2
RETURN
```

THE SUBROUTINE DPRTOUT

The last subroutine required for decipherment is appropriately
labeled DPRTOUT to reflect the fact that it prints the results of the
decipherment process. Unlike the subroutine PRTOUT, which
limited the number of characters to 25 per line and required
extensive logic to operate on strings and invoke the GROUPBY5
subroutine, DPRTOUT is very simple. DPRTOUT simply reads
each line in the file containing the deciphered message, eliminates any slash character used as a line prefix, and prints each
line as is (Listing 2.19 contains the contents of this subroutine).

Listing 2.19. The subroutine DPRTOUT.

```
DPRTOUT: REM Subroutine to print results
        INPUT "Press Return key to display resulting enciphered
➥message," p$
        CLS
        PRINT "Resulting deciphered message is:"
        OPEN OUTFILE$ FOR INPUT AS #2
        DO UNTIL EOF(2)
                INPUT #2, TEXT$
                IF MID$(TEXT$, 1, 1) = "/" THEN PRINT
➥RIGHT$(TEXT$, LEN(TEXT$) - 1)
```

```
                IF MID$(TEXT$, 1, 1) <> "/" THEN PRINT TEXT$
        LOOP
RETURN
```

To illustrate the composition of the resulting decipherment program, Listing 2.20 contains the main portion of the program DCIPHER4.BAS. You should note that two of the five subroutines, INITIALIZE and FORMCIPHER, are exactly the same as those subroutines used in CIPHER4.BAS. The three remaining subroutines, DMSGFILE, DECIPHER, and DPRTOUT are modified versions of the subroutines MSGFILE, CONVERTSTORE, and PRTOUT. The entire decipherment program that deciphers a message enciphered using a simple monoalphabetic substitution process is stored on the file DCIPHER4.BAS on the convenience disk.

Listing 2.20. The main portion of the DCIPHER4.BAS program.

```
REM PROGRAM DCIPHER4.BAS
DIM PLAINTEXT$(26), CIPHERTEXT$(26)
CLS

GOSUB INITIALIZE
        PRINT "DCIPHER4.BAS PROGRAM deciphers a message using a
➡simple"
        PRINT "monoalphabetic substitution process."
1       INPUT "Enter UPPERCASE Alphabetic Shift Key: ", K$
        FOR I = 0 TO 25
        IF K$ = PLAINTEXT$(I) GOTO 2
        NEXT I
        PRINT "You must enter a letter from A to Z"
        GOTO 1
2       REM Position I represents shift key letter
GOSUB FORMCIPHER                'create cipher alphabet
GOSUB DMSGFILE                  'assign I/O files, place message on a
                                ➡file
GOSUB DECIPHER                  'convert enciphered message to plaintext
GOSUB DPRTOUT                   'print results
END
```

PROGRAM EXECUTION

To illustrate the operation of the DCIPHER4.BAS program, you can execute the program with input from the keyboard and from a file. To facilitate a comparison of the deciphered message to the original plaintext message, you can use the enciphered message contained at the bottom of Listing 2.15 as input to DCIPHER4.BAS.

Listing 2.21 illustrates the operation of DCIPHER4.BAS in which keyboard input was selected. In this example, you must use the keyboard to enter the ciphertext message in the same manner as it was displayed as a result of the execution of CIPHER4.BAS. That is, you must prefix each cleartext line with a slash, enter each line using the 5-character groups contained on the line, and terminate the enciphered message with a backslash character on a separate line.

Listing 2.21. The execution of DCIPHER4.BAS using keyboard input.

```
DCIPHER4.BAS PROGRAM deciphers a message using a simple
monoalphabetic substitution process.
Enter UPPERCASE Alphabetic Shift Key: B
Enter filename to store enciphered message, default=CIPHERTX.DAT
Enter filename to store deciphered message, default=MESSAGE.DAT
Select keyboard (k) or file (f) ciphertext message input: K
Enter your message - place a / at the beginning of each line
that should remain in plaintext and a \ on a separate line
to indicate the end of the enciphered message

/TO ALL BRANCH CHIEFS
/FROM PRESIDENT V.F. SMALL
FWGVQ VJGRT GUGPV UVCVG QHVJG
GEQPQ OAYGO WUVVG TOKPC VGVYG
PVARG TEGPV QHQWT GORNQ AGGUD
APGZV HTKFC AUVQR AQWOW UVRTG
RCTGA QWTJK VNKUV VJKUY GGMGP
```

```
FCPFV TCPUO KVVJC VNKUV KPGPE
KRJGT GFHQT OVQOG DAPKP GCOOQ
PFCAU VQRXX
\
Press Return key to display resulting enciphered message


Resulting deciphered message is:
TO ALL BRANCH CHIEFS
FROM PRESIDENT V.F. SMALL
DUETOTHEPRESENTSTATEOFTHE
ECONOMYWEMUSTTERMINATETWE
NTYPERCENTOFOUREMPLOYEESB
YNEXTFRIDAYSTOPYOUMUSTPRE
PAREYOURHITLISTTHISWEEKEN
DANDTRANSMITTHATLISTINENC
IPHEREDFORMTOMEBYNINEAMMO
NDAYSTOPVV
```

The execution of DCIPHER4.BAS using keyboard input displays up to 25 characters per line because input is limited to five groups of 5 characters per line. In comparison, the use of file input when DCIPHER4.BAS (see Listing 2.22) is executed deciphers each full line contained on the file whose name was assigned to the variable OUTFILE$. The use of file input may provide you with a more natural conversion to plaintext because words do not have to be split among two lines if they do not fit into a 5-character group terminating a line.

Listing 2.22. The execution of DCIPHER4.BAS using file input.

```
DCIPHER4.BAS PROGRAM deciphers a message using a simple
monoalphabetic substitution process.
Enter UPPERCASE Alphabetic Shift Key: B
Enter filename to store enciphered message, default=CIPHERTX.DAT
Enter filename to store deciphered message, default=MESSAGE.DAT
```

continues

Listing 2.22. Continued

```
Select keyboard (k) or file (f) ciphertext message input: F
Press Return key to display resulting enciphered message


Resulting deciphered message is:
TO ALL BRANCH CHIEFS
FROM PRESIDENT V.F. SMALL
DUETOTHEPRESENTSTATEOFTHEECONOMYWEMUSTTERMINATE
TWENTYPERCENTOFOUREMPLOYEESBYNEXTFRIDAYSTOP
YOUMUSTPREPAREYOURHITLISTTHISWEEKENDANDTRANSMIT
THATLISTINENCIPHEREDFORMTOMEBYNINEAMMONDAYSTOP
```

3

KEYWORD-BASED MONOALPHABETIC SUBSTITUTION

Using the information presented in Chapter 2, "Monoalphabetic Substitution Concepts," as a base, this chapter continues the examination of monoalphabetic substitution techniques. This discussion opens with the development and use of a keyword-based, mixed alphabet to add a degree of randomness to the development of plaintext and ciphertext alphabets. Several additional techniques that can be used to develop a ciphertext alphabet are also covered in this chapter. As in Chapter 2, you will examine different techniques and develop a series of subroutines and programs in Microsoft Corporation's QuickBASIC to automate the operation of each technique.

KEYWORD-BASED MIXED ALPHABETS

The relationship between plaintext and ciphertext alphabets in which one alphabet is shifted from the other by n positions is easy to construct. Unfortunately, this system also offers a limited degree of message protection. To add an additional level of protection, keyword-based, mixed alphabets were developed.

CONSTRUCTION

In a keyword-based, mixed alphabet, a word or phrase is selected as the keyword and used for the formation of the letters of the alphabet (repeated letters are omitted after their first occurrence). At the end of the word or phrase, the remaining letters of the alphabet are used in their normal sequence, omitting letters previously used in the keyword or phrase. For example, suppose you use the phrase GOD SAVE THE QUEEN as a keyword phrase. The first step in this process is to group the phrase to form one word and eliminate duplicate letters in this newly formed word—GODSAVETHQUN. Add the remaining letters of the alphabet to the end of the keyword to give you the keyword-based, mixed alphabet GODSAVETHQUNBCFIJKLMPRWXYZ.

AUTOMATING KEYWORD CONSTRUCTION

Listing 3.1 illustrates the statements in the program WORD.BAS that (when executed) produce a keyword-based, mixed-sequence alphabet. This program contains two subroutines: INITIALIZE and KEYWORD. The first subroutine is the same subroutine used in the CIPHER series of programs developed in Chapter 2 to initialize the PLAINTEXT array. The second subroutine was developed to produce a keyword-based, mixed-sequence alphabet. In this section, the focus is upon the KEYWORD subroutine, which actually forms the keyword-based, mixed-sequence alphabet. After a review of the operation of this subroutine, I'll show you how to incorporate it into a new series of programs that enable you to create keyword-based, mixed-sequence alphabets as plaintext and ciphertext alphabets and to incorporate a shift key character to encipher a message.

Listing 3.1. The WORD.BAS program listing.

```
REM PROGRAM WORD.BAS TO DEVELOP ALPHABET BASED ON A KEYWORD
DIM PLAINTEXT$(26), CIPHERTEXT$(26), KEY$(26)
        GOSUB INITIALIZE
        INPUT "Enter keyword in CAPS ", TEXT$
        GOSUB KEYWORD
```

```
            PRINT "Keyword-based alphabet is: "; X$
            STOP
INITIALIZE:
            REM Initialize plaintext values
            FOR I = 0 TO 25
            READ PLAINTEXT$(I)
            NEXT I
            DATA "A","B","C","D","E","F","G","H","I","J","K","L","M","N"
            DATA "O","P","Q","R","S","T","U","V","W","X","Y","Z"
RETURN
KEYWORD:
            REM Place entered keyword into KEY$ array 1 character per
          ➥position
                MSGLEN = LEN(TEXT$)
                FOR I = 1 TO MSGLEN
                KEY$(I) = MID$(TEXT$, I, 1)
                NEXT I
            REM ELIMINATE DUPLICATE LETTERS, REPLACE WITH NULLS
                K = 2
                FOR I = 1 TO MSGLEN
                FOR J = K TO MSGLEN
                IF KEY$(I) <> KEY$(J) GOTO NOTDUP
                KEY$(J) = " "
NOTDUP:         NEXT J
                K = K + 1
                NEXT I
            REM REMOVE NULLS IN STRING
                X$ = ""
                FOR I = 1 TO MSGLEN
                X$ = X$ + LTRIM$(KEY$(I))
                NEXT I
            REM PLACE REVISED KEYWORD WITH NO DUPLICATE LETTERS BACK IN
          ➥KEY$
                FOR I = 1 TO LEN(X$)
                KEY$(I) = MID$(X$, I, 1)
                NEXT I
            REM COMPARE KEY$ & PLAINTEXT$ ARRAYS, BLANK PLAINTEXT$ WHEN
          ➥MATCHED
```

continues

Listing 3.1. Continued

```
                    FOR J = 1 TO LEN(X$)
                    FOR K = 0 TO 25
                    IF KEY$(J) = PLAINTEXT$(K) THEN PLAINTEXT$(K) =
                    ➥" "
                    NEXT K
                    NEXT J
        REM CREATE ONE STRING
                    FOR I = 0 TO 25
                    X$ = X$ + LTRIM$(PLAINTEXT$(I))
                    NEXT I
        REM PLACE SEQUENCE BACK INTO PLAINTEXT$ ARRAY
                    FOR I = 0 TO 25
                    PLAINTEXT$(I) = MID$(X$, I + 1, 1)
                    NEXT I
RETURN
END
```

The use of a mnemonic key to mix a cipher alphabet can be traced to a family of cryptologists that lived in Rome during the sixteenth century. One member of this family, Matteo Argenti, served as the Papal secretary of ciphers under Pope Gregory XIV and five succeeding popes. Argenti taught cryptology to his younger brother, Marcello, who served as a cipher secretary to a cardinal and wrote a cryptology manual that contained the first written reference to the use of a mnemonic key to mix a cipher alphabet.

The first keyword-mixed alphabet developed by Argenti used numerics in place of ciphertext characters. To increase the difficulty of unauthorized decipherment operations, the letters q and u were merged into a single unit for encipherment, and rules prohibiting word separations and punctuation were developed.

THE SUBROUTINE KEYWORD

It may be useful to review the operation of the subroutine
KEYWORD based on each group of statements bounded by a REM
statement. The first program module simply stores each character in the keyword into an element of the KEY$ string array. The
second program module uses a nested pair of FOR-NEXT loops to
eliminate duplicate letters in the keyword, replacing each duplicate letter with a null character. To illustrate the operation of
this program module, assume that the keyword ALPHA was used
and that it has a string length of 5. In the program module, the
inner loop (J) operates from 2 to 5, and the outer loop operates
from 1 to 5. Thus, when I is 1, J varies from 2 to 5. This results in
A being compared to L, P, H, and A. If KEY$(I) does not equal
KEY$(J), a branch to the label NOTDUP occurs and J is incremented.
If KEY$(I) equals KEY$(J), the statement KEY$(J)=" " sets KEY$(J) as
equal to a null character. After the value of J increments, K is
incremented, which results in the second character in the
keyword (L) being compared to the third (P) through the fifth
(A) characters of the keyword.

The third program module removes the nulls previously
inserted in place of duplicate characters. The statement
X$=X$+LTRIM$(KEY$(I)) concatenates each element of KEY$ that is
non-null with the previous value of X$ because the string func-
tion LTRIM$ removes leading nulls from a string.

The fourth program module takes the recently formed string
variable X$, which contains the keyword without duplicate
characters, and places those characters back into the array KEY$.
The fifth program module then compares each character in the
KEY$ array to each character in the PLAINTEXT$ array. If they
match, the plaintext character is set to a null. The sixth program
module simply adds each nonblank element position of the
PLAINTEXT array to the string X$, which now contains the keyword-
based, mixed alphabet. The seventh program module places the
keyword-based alphabet into the array PLAINTEXT$.

 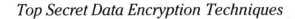

The use of the previously described WORD.BAS program is illustrated in Listing 3.2, which demonstrates the QuickBASIC execution screen after the program WORD.BAS was executed three times in succession. The first time WORD.BAS is executed the keyword phrase SEVENBRIDES is used to develop the keyword-based, mixed alphabet. The second time the program is executed the keyword phrase BROOKLYNBRIDGE is used. The third keyword phrase is MICROSOFTWINDOWSISGREAT.

Listing 3.2. The results obtained from executing WORD.BAS several times.

```
Enter keyword in CAPS:       SEVENBRIDES
Keyword-based alphabet is:   SEVNBRIDACFGHJKLMOPQTUWXYZ
Enter keyword in CAPS:       BROOKLYNBRIDGE
Keyword-based alphabet is:   BROKLYNIDGEACFHJMPQSTUVWXZ
Enter keyword in CAPS:       MICROSOFTWINDOWSISGREAT
Keyword-based alphabet is:   MICROSFTWNDGEABHJKLPQUVXYZ
```

You should note that the trailing portions of the resulting alphabets are very similar. In fact, the characters U and Z are positioned at the same locations in each alphabet.

If you simply positioned a keyword-based alphabet directly under a plaintext alphabet there is a high degree of probability that one or more plaintext and ciphertext characters would equate. This situation would obviously provide a valuable clue to the decipherment of an intercepted message. To eliminate or reduce the number of coincidental characters between a plaintext alphabet and a keyword-based, ciphertext alphabet, you need to apply an alphabetic shift key to one or both alphabets.

INCORPORATING AN ALPHABETIC SHIFT KEY

In Chapter 2, you developed a program (CIPHER4.BAS) that creates enciphered text based on the use of an alphabetic shift key. In this chapter, the discussion of monoalphabetic

substitution is continued by examining the development of a keyword-based, mixed alphabet and the statements in a subroutine contained in the program WORD.BAS to automate the keyword-based, mixed alphabet creation process. Combining the use of a keyword-based, mixed alphabet with an alphabetic shift key should result in a higher level of enciphered data protection. Thus, this section focuses on combining both techniques for enciphering and deciphering messages.

By placing the KEYWORD subroutine contained in WORD.BAS into the CIPHER4.BAS program, you gain the ability to encipher a message based upon a keyword or keyword phrase and an alphabetic shift. I'll call the new program CIPHER5.BAS.

THE CIPHER5.BAS PROGRAM

Listing 3.3 illustrates the statements contained in the main portion of CIPHER5.BAS as well as the subroutine INITIALIZE, which required a slight modification. You should note that lines terminating with five asterisks (*) as a comment indicate lines that were added to the main program to facilitate an explanation of its operation. Those lines can be removed if you do not wish to burden a user who has no desire to understand the enciphering process with this extraneous information.

Listing 3.3. The main portion of the program CIPHER5.BAS and the modified subroutine INITIALIZE.

```
REM PROGRAM CIPHER5.BAS
DIM PLAINTEXT$(26), CIPHERTEXT$(26), KEY$(26)
CLS
GOSUB INITIALIZE
        PRINT "CIPHER5.BAS PROGRAM enciphers text based upon the use
        ➼of a keyword or keyword"
        PRINT "phrase and an alphabetic shift key using a
        ➼monoalphabetic substitution process."
        PRINT
        INPUT "Enter keyword or keyword phrase in UPPERCASE: ", TEXT$
        PRINT "Plaintext based alphabet is              : ";
        ➼'*****
```

continues

Listing 3.3. Continued

```
          FOR I = 0 TO 25: PRINT PLAINTEXT$(I); : NEXT I  '*****
          ➥GOSUB KEYWORD                          'form keyword-based mixed
                                                  ➥alphabet
          PRINT "Keyword-based alphabet is : "; X$      '*****
1         INPUT "Enter UPPERCASE Alphabetic Shift Key: ", K$
          FOR I = 0 TO 25
          IF K$ = PLAINTEXT$(I) GOTO 2
          NEXT I
          PRINT "You must enter a letter from A to Z"
          GOTO 1
2         REM Position I represents shift key letter

GOSUB FORMCIPHER                      'create cipher alphabet
          PRINT "Shifted keyword mixed alphabet is : ";  '*****
          ➥FOR I = 0 TO 25: PRINT CIPHERTEXT$(I); : NEXT I: PRINT
          ➥'*****
GOSUB INITIALIZE                      'reinitialize plaintext array
GOSUB MSGFILE                         'assign I/O files, place message on a
                                      ➥file
GOSUB CONVERTSTORE                    'convert and store ciphertext on a file
GOSUB PRTOUT                          'print results
STOP
INITIALIZE:
          RESTORE
          REM Initialize plaintext values
          FOR I = 0 TO 25
          READ PLAINTEXT$(I)
          NEXT I
          DATA "A","B","C","D","E","F","G","H","I","J","K","L","M","N"
          DATA "O","P","Q","R","S","T","U","V","W","X","Y","Z"
RETURN
```

As indicated in Listing 3.3, first initialize the string array
PLAINTEXT$ and then display information about the program.
After the keyword or keyword phrase is entered and assigned
to the string variable TEXT$, the plaintext alphabet is displayed.

The subroutine KEYWORD is now invoked to form a keyword-based, mixed alphabet. This subroutine is the same as the subroutine developed in the program WORD.BAS.

After the subroutine KEYWORD is invoked, the keyword-based alphabet is displayed through the use of another optional statement. The user is then prompted to enter an alphabetic shift character, and the subroutine FORMCIPHER is invoked to create a cipher alphabet. That alphabet is displayed through the use of a pair of optional statements.

Because the subroutine FORMCIPHER creates the cipher alphabet by shifting the previously created keyword-based, mixed alphabet, you must restore the plaintext alphabet to its original sequence to correctly convert plaintext characters to their equivalent ciphertext characters. This is accomplished by again invoking the subroutine INITIALIZE. However, because that subroutine previously read the normal letter sequence into the array PLAINTEXT, you must place a RESTORE statement at the beginning of the subroutine—if RESTORE isn't placed, an "out-of-data" error message appears.

THE ENCIPHERMENT PROCESS

Listing 3.4 illustrates the execution of CIPHER5.BAS to encipher a short but important message. To understand the encipherment process, examine the composition of the different alphabets displayed by the program.

Listing 3.4. A sample execution of CIPHER5.BAS.

```
CIPHER5.BAS PROGRAM enciphers text based upon the use of a
➥keyword or keyword phrase and an alphabetic shift key using a
➥monoalphabetic substitution process.

Enter keyword or keyword phrase in UPPERCASE: MICROSOFTWINDOWS
Plaintext-based alphabet is  : ABCDEFGHIJKLMNOPQRSTUVWXYZ
Keyword-based alphabet is  : MICROSFTWNDABEGHJKLPQUVXYZ
```

continues

Listing 3.4. Continued

```
Enter UPPERCASE Alphabetic Shift Key: B
Shifted keyword mixed alphabet is              :
➡EGHJKLPQUVXYZMICROSFTWNDAB
Enter filename to store plaintext message, default=MESSAGE.DAT
Enter filename to store enciphered message, default=CIPHERTX.DAT
Select keyboard (k) or file (f) message input: K
Enter your message - place a / at the beginning of each line
that should remain in plaintext and a \ on a separate line
to indicate the end of the enciphered message


/TO: JOHN P. BIDDER
/FROM: PRESIDENT V.F. SMALL
BID NO MORE THAN TWO HUNDRED THOUSAND FOR THE PROPERTY
\
Press Return key to display resulting enciphered message




Resulting enciphered message is:
TO: JOHN P. BIDDER
FROM: PRESIDENT V.F. SMALL
GUJMI ZIOKF QEMFN IQTMJ OKJFK
MFQIT SEMJL IOFQK COICK OFAXX
```

The plaintext-based alphabet is simply the character sequence A through Z. After a keyword or keyword phrase is entered, the plaintext sequence is modified based on the keyword or keyword phrase. For example, entering the keyword MICROSOFTWINDOWS results in the keyword-based alphabet MICROSFTWNDABEGHJKLPQUVXYZ because all duplicate characters in the keyword or keyword phrase are eliminated prior to the addition of the characters in the plaintext alphabet that are not in the modified keyword or keyword phrase.
The entry of an alphabetic shift key causes the cycling of the keyword-based alphabet so that all characters to and including the alphabetic shift key character are rotated. Thus, the shifted-keyword, mixed alphabet becomes EGHJKLPQUVXYZMICROSFTWNDAB.

The encipherment process requires each character in the message to be located in the array PLAINTEXT$, which contains the normal alphabetic sequence. When a match is found, the ciphertext character located in the same position in the shifted-keyword, mixed alphabet in the CIPHERTEXT$ array is extracted and substituted for the plaintext character. Note the positional relationship of characters between the plaintext-based alphabet and the shifted-keyword, mixed alphabet in Listing 3.4. The first character in the message is B, located in the second position in the plaintext alphabet. The second character in the shifted-keyword, mixed alphabet is G (B was replaced by G). The second letter in the message is I, located in the ninth position in the plaintext alphabet. In the ninth position in the shifted-keyword, mixed alphabet, extract a U. Similarly, D is replaced by the character J, and the first word in the plaintext message, BID, is enciphered as GUJ.

DECIPHERING OPERATIONS

After developing CIPHER5.BAS, it's only logical that a mechanism is required to restore a received message to its original plaintext content. In this section, several previously developed subroutines are modified and incorporated into a program appropriately named DCIPHER5.BAS, which performs the inverse function of CIPHER5.BAS. Although you could incorporate deciphering operations into CIPHER5.BAS, it is easier to explain deciphering coding operations as a separate entity. In addition, some organizations may prefer to limit certain corporate locations' capability to decipher or encipher messages. Thus, the separation of enciphering and deciphering operations may be preferred by some users. For other users who prefer a program that combines both operations, I'll develop some programs using more sophisticated enciphering techniques later in this book. However, because the focus is on the development of modular routines, I will show you the ease in which modules from both programs can be combined.

Prior to developing the coding required to decipher a message created through the use of a keyword or keyword phrase and an alphabetic shift, it may be useful to review the manual process required to decipher a message enciphered in this manner.

THE DECIPHERMENT PROCESS

To correctly decipher an enciphered message developed using a keyword or keyword phrase and a shift key requires knowledge of both elements. Once both elements are known, you can construct a keyword-based, mixed alphabet and shift the alphabet to obtain the cipher alphabet. To initiate the deciphering process, place the cipher alphabet above the plaintext alphabet. For each letter in the enciphered message, locate its position in the cipher alphabet and extract the plaintext character at the position in the alphabet that equals the position of the enciphered character in the cipher alphabet. For example, assume that the keyword phrase is GODSAVETHEQUEEN and that the shift key is the character B. In this case, the keyword-based alphabet becomes GODSAVETHQUNBCFIJKLMPRWXYZ. Because the shift key is the character B, shift the keyword-based alphabet until it is positioned so that the character B is on the extreme right. Remember that the alphabetic shift key was previously defined as an uppercase character in the plaintext alphabet that defines the location where the right end of the resulting shifted alphabet ends. Thus, using the shift key character B results in the cipher alphabet CFIJKLMPRWXYZGODSAVETHQUNB.

Now that you have constructed the cipher alphabet based on the predefined keyword phrase and shift key, place that alphabet above the plaintext alphabet:

cipher alphabet: CFIJKLMPRWXYZGODSAVETHQUNB
plaintext alphabet: ABCDEFGHIJKLMNOPQRSTUVWXYZ

Now suppose the first two groups of five enciphered characters in a received message are LRAKU OVKDP. Searching the cipher alphabet, locate the character L and read down the same position into the plaintext alphabet to extract the character F. Similarly, R in the cipher alphabet corresponds to I in the plaintext, A corresponds to R in the plaintext alphabet, K in the cipher alphabet corresponds to E in the plaintext alphabet, and so on. Thus, LRAKU OVKDP is equivalent to FIREJOSEPH in plaintext.

THE DCIPHER5.BAS PROGRAM

To automate deciphering of an enciphered message based on the use of a keyword or keyword phrase and an alphabetic shift key, I'll construct a program appropriately named DCIPHER5.BAS. To do this, I'll use all of the previously developed subroutines included in CIPHER5.BAS as is or in a slightly modified form. To indicate that a change was made to a previously developed subroutine, I will prefix its name with the character D to indicate its modification for a decipherment operation.

Listing 3.5 contains the statements that make up the main portion of DCIPHER5.BAS. Similar to the statements in CIPHER5.BAS, a comment of five asterisks is used to denote a PRINT statement included for illustrative purposes (eliminating these statements does not affect the operation of the program).

Listing 3.5. The main portion of DCIPHER5.BAS program.

```
REM PROGRAM DCIPHER5.BAS
DIM PLAINTEXT$(26), CIPHERTEXT$(26), KEY$(26)
CLS
GOSUB INITIALIZE
PRINT "DCIPHER5.BAS PROGRAM deciphers text based upon
       ➡the use of a keyword or keyword"
       PRINT "phrase and an alphabetic shift key using a
       ➡monoalphabetic substitution process."
```

continues

Listing 3.5. Continued

```
          PRINT
          INPUT "Enter keyword or keyword phrase in UPPERCASE: ",
          ➥TEXT$
          PRINT "Plaintext-based alphabet is : "; '*****
          FOR I = 0 TO 25: PRINT PLAINTEXT$(I); : NEXT I '*****
          GOSUB KEYWORD                      'form keyword-based mixed
                                             ➥alphabet
          PRINT "Keyword-based alphabet is : "; X$ '*****
1         INPUT "Enter UPPERCASE Alphabetic Shift Key: ", K$
          FOR I = 0 TO 25
          IF K$ = PLAINTEXT$(I) GOTO 2
          NEXT I
          PRINT "You must enter a letter from A to Z"
          GOTO 1
2         REM Position I represents shift key letter

GOSUB FORMCIPHER                     'create cipher alphabet
          PRINT "Shifted keyword mixed alphabet is : "; '*****
          FOR I = 0 TO 25: PRINT CIPHERTEXT$(I); : NEXT I: PRINT
          ➥ '*****
GOSUB INITIALIZE                     'reinitialize plaintext array
GOSUB DMSGFILE                       'assign I/O files, place message on
                                     ➥a file
GOSUB DCONVERTSTORE                  'convert and store plaintext on a
                                     ➥file
GOSUB PRTOUT                         'print results
STOP
```

It should be noted that the only difference between the main portion of CIPHER5.BAS and DCIPHER5.BAS (other than changing the description of the program) is the subroutine names DMSGFILE and DCONVERTSTORE.

THE SUBROUTINE DMSGFILE

The process of assigning I/O files must be reversed for decipherment—the filename used for the input of the plaintext message
in the CIPHER5.BAS program becomes the output file. Similarly,
the filename used for the storage of the enciphered message in
the CIPHER5.BAS program becomes the input file for decipherment operations. To provide those modifications you must
change the use of the string variables OUTFILE$ and INFILE$ previously used in the subroutine MSGFILE. To change I/O file assignments, simply reverse the use of the previously mentioned
string variables.

Listing 3.6 lists the statements in the new subroutine named
DMSGFILE, which contains the reversal of I/O file assignments.
If you compare this subroutine to the previously developed
subroutine MSGFILE you should note that the difference between the two is limited to the previously mentioned reversal
of I/O filename assignments.

Listing 3.6. The subroutine DMSGFILE.

```
DMSGFILE:
        REM Routine to assign I/O files and accept keyboard or file
        ➥input
        REM and remove spaces between words
                INPUT "Enter filename to store plaintext message,
                    default=MESSAGE.DAT", OUTFILE$
                IF OUTFILE$ = "" THEN OUTFILE$ = "MESSAGE.DAT"
                INPUT "Enter filename for enciphered message,
                    default=CIPHERTX.DAT", infile$
                IF INFILE$ = "" THEN INFILE$ = "CIPHERTX.DAT"
                INPUT "Select keyboard (k) or file (f) message input:
                  ➥", IN$
                IF IN$ = "F" OR IN$ = "f" THEN RETURN
                OPEN INFILE$ FOR OUTPUT AS #1
```

continues

Listing 3.6. Continued

```
             REM Routine to place message on a file removing spaces
          ➥between words
                PRINT "Enter your message - place a / at the
                ➥beginning of each line"
                PRINT "that should remain in plaintext and a \ on a
                ➥separate line"
                PRINT "to indicate the end of the enciphered message"
                PRINT
AGN:            LINE INPUT TEXT$
                IF MID$(TEXT$, 1, 1) = "/" THE GOTO XT
                NTEXT$ = ""
                FOR I = 1 TO LEN(TEXT$)
                NTEXT$ = NTEXT$ + LTRIM$(MID$(TEXT$, I, 1))
                NEXT I
                WRITE #1, NTEXT$
                IF MID$(TEXT$, 1, 1) = "\" GOTO DONE
                GOTO AGN
XT:             WRITE #1, TEXT$
                GOTO AGN
DONE:              CLOSE #1
RETURN
```

THE SUBROUTINE DCONVERTSTORE

The second subroutine that requires modification for deciphering is CONVERTSTORE. (As discussed, the modified subroutine was renamed DCONVERTSTORE to reflect its modification for decipherment operations.)

Listing 3.7 contains the statements found in the subroutine DCONVERTSTORE. Other than changing two REM statements to reflect the fact that the routine now converts ciphertext to plaintext, the only additional changes relate to search-and-replacement operations. The IF statement in the nested FOR-NEXT loop now compares each character in the string variable TEXT$

to each character in the CIPHERTEXT$ array instead of the PLAINTEXT$ array. When a match occurs, the character in TEXT$ is replaced by a character in the array PLAINTEXT$ located at the same position in the array where the character in TEXT$ matched the character in the array CIPHERTEXT$. Thus, DCONVERTSTORE simply makes use of the use of the plaintext alphabet stored in the array PLAINTEXT$ and the ciphertext alphabet stored in the array CIPHERTEXT$ in the reverse manner in which they were used in the subroutine CONVERTSTORE.

Listing 3.7. The DCONVERTSTORE subroutine.

```
DCONVERTSTORE:
        REM Routine to convert and store plaintext on a file
        OPEN INFILE$ FOR INPUT AS #1
        OPEN OUTFILE$ FOR OUTPUT AS #2
        DO UNTIL EOF(1)
                INPUT #1, TEXT$
                MSGLEN = LEN(TEXT$)
                IF MID$(TEXT$, 1, 1) = "/" THEN GOTO CLEARTXT
                IF MID$(TEXT$, 1, 1) = "\" THEN GOTO DONE1
                REM Convert ciphertext to plaintext
                        FOR I = 1 TO MSGLEN
                        FOR J = 0 TO 25
                        IF MID$(TEXT$, I, 1) = CIPHERTEXT$(J)
                        ➡THEN GOTO GOTIT
                        NEXT J
GOTIT:                  MID$(TEXT$, I, 1) = PLAINTEXT$(J)
                        NEXT I
CLEARTXT:               WRITE #2, TEXT$
        LOOP
DONE1:          CLOSE #2
        RETURN
```

PROGRAM OPERATION

To illustrate the operation of the DCIPHER5.BAS program, you can execute it using the previously enciphered message to the

fictional JOHN P. BINDER as input. Regardless of whether you use the keyboard or specify a file for input of the ciphered messaged, the program produces the same result. Listing 3.8 illustrates the execution of DCIPHER5.BAS in which the keyboard is used to enter the received enciphered message. Because the previously developed subroutine PRTOUT was used to display the resulting deciphered message, that message is displayed in groups of five characters as indicated in the lower portion of Listing 3.8. Although the program converted the ciphertext message back into its plaintext character representation, it did not restore the message to its original format with spaces between words and words rebuilt from two or more five-character groupings when it crossed such groupings. Those functions cannot be performed when the encipherment method does not substitute a character for the space character (the recipient of the deciphered message must understand how to correctly read the deciphered message).

Listing 3.8. The execution of DCIPHER5.BAS.

```
DCIPHER5.BAS PROGRAM deciphers text based upon the use of a
➥keyword or keyword phrase and an alphabetic shift key using a
➥monoalphabetic substitution process.


Enter keyword or keyword phrase in UPPERCASE: MICROSOFTWINDOWS
Plaintext-based alphabet is : ABCDEFGHIJKLMNOPQRSTUVWXYZ
Keyword-based alphabet is :   MICROSFTWNDABEGHJKLPQUVXYZ
Enter UPPERCASE Alphabetic Shift Key: B
Shifted keyword mixed alphabet is : EGHJKLPQUVXYZMICROSFTWNDAB
Enter filename to store plaintext message, default=MESSAGE.DAT
Enter filename to store enciphered message, default=CIPHERTX.DAT
Select keyboard (k) or file (f) message input: K
Enter your message - place a / at the beginning of each line
that should remain in plaintext and a \ on a separate line
to indicate the end of the enciphered message


/TO: JOHN P. BINDER
CUJMI ZIOKF QEMFN IQTMJ OKJFK
MFQIT SEMJL IOFQK COICK OFAXX

\
```

```
Press Return key to display resulting deciphered message


Resulting deciphered message is:
TO JOHN P. BINDER
BIDNO MORET HANTW OHUND REDTE
NTHOU SANDF ORTHE PROPE RTYKK
```

ALTERNATIVE RELATIONSHIPS

Up to this point, the focus has been on using the development of a keyword-based, mixed alphabet to create a ciphertext alphabet. Once this was accomplished, an alphabetic shift key was used to further mix the relationship between plaintext and ciphertext alphabets. In performing those tasks the only information a message recipient requires is the keyword or keyword phrase and the alphabetic shift key to decipher a message through the use of a program. With a little knowledge of the method used to create a keyword-based, mixed alphabet and the use of a shift key, most people can learn how to manually decipher a message. The major benefit of the previously described encipherment method is the ability of most people to manually perform encipherment and decipherment with a minimum of information.

You can extend the use of keyword or keyword phrase mixed alphabets and alphabetic shifting to the plaintext alphabet. In fact, you can develop the nine common alphabetic relationships listed in Table 3.1. You could also reverse the resulting plaintext, ciphertext, or both plaintext and ciphertext alphabets to increase the number of alphabetic relationships. However, this may add a degree of confusion to both encipherment and decipherment due to the large number of options users could be forced to consider and remember. To keep your techniques practical, however, I'll simply illustrate the use of two keyword-based mixed-sequence alphabets for enciphering a message and leave it to you to modify CIPHER5.BAS to obtain other plaintext-ciphertext relationships.

Table 3.1.
Common alphabet relationships.

plaintext alphabet in normal sequence	ciphertext alphabet in normal sequence and shifted
plaintext alphabet in normal sequence	ciphertext alphabet in keyword mixed sequence
plaintext alphabet in normal sequence	ciphertext alphabet in keyword mixed sequence and shifted
plaintext alphabet in keyword mixed sequence	ciphertext alphabet in normal sequence and shifted
plaintext alphabet in keyword mixed sequence	ciphertext alphabet in keyword mixed sequence
plaintext alphabet in keyword mixed sequence	ciphertext alphabet in keyword mixed sequence and shifted
plaintext alphabet in keyword mixed sequence and shifted	ciphertext alphabet in normal sequence and shifted
plaintext alphabet in keyword mixed sequence and shifted	ciphertext alphabet in keyword mixed sequence
plaintext alphabet in keyword mixed sequence and shifted	ciphertext alphabet in keyword mixed sequence and shifted

To illustrate the use of two keyword-based, mixed alphabets, assume the keyword SANDIEGO is used to form the plaintext alphabet and the keyword BALTIMORE is used to form the ciphertext alphabet. Table 3.2 illustrates the resulting mixed plaintext and ciphertext alphabets.

Table 3.2.
Dual mixed alphabet relationship.

Plaintext keyword	SANDIEGO
Ciphertext keyword	BALTIMORE
Mixed plaintext alphabet:	SANDIEGOBCFHJKLMPQRTUVWXYZ
Mixed ciphertext alphabet:	BALTIMORECDFGHJKNPQSUVWXYZ

If you wish to encode BID, perform the same operation—locate B in the mixed plaintext alphabet and note its position. Then extract the character in the ciphertext alphabet that corresponds to the location of B in the plaintext alphabet (B is replaced by E). Then locate the letter I in the mixed plaintext alphabet; the letter I should be extracted from the ciphertext alphabet. Similarly, D should be replaced by T.

Sometimes luck works both ways. During World War I, the British War Office developed a cipher device that they planned to distribute to British forces as a field cipher. So highly regarded was the device that one argument against its adoption for field use was its possible capture and use by the Germans—a situation many high-level personnel in the Allied forces thought would preclude the ability of the Allies to decipher enemy messages. To verify the security of their device, the British submitted five short enciphered messages to the only formal cryptologic organization in the United States.

Located on a 500-acre estate named Riverbank at Geneva, Illinois, the Department of Ciphers at Riverbank was headed by William Frederick Friedman, considered by some to be America's greatest cryptologist. Although Friedman was able to determine the keyword of one of the mixed alphabets, apparently he hit the proverbial "blank wall" with the other keyword. Turning to his wife, he asked her to clear her mind and tell him the first word that came to mind when he said a word. When he said the first keyword, CIPHER, she replied

continues

continued

"machine." This intuitive guess was correct, and Friedman cabled the plaintext solution to the five messages to London, dooming the adoption of the device many persons were afraid would, if captured by the Germans, preclude the Allies from solving enemy messages.

WEAKNESS

Note that although two different keywords were used, many characters in the ciphertext alphabet are the same as their plaintext equivalents, especially towards the end of each alphabet. This is one of several weaknesses of mixed alphabets. A long message may provide numerous hints when ciphertext and plaintext characters coincide. It is more practical to use one keyword-based alphabet and an appropriate alphabetic shift key to eliminate the overlapping of plaintext and ciphertext characters than to simply use two keyword mixed alphabets.

The second major weakness of all keyword-based monoalphabetic substitution techniques is the fact that a continuous one-for-one character replacement forms the basis of this category of enciphering techniques. This means that these techniques are vulnerable to decipherment by a person performing a frequency analysis of characters in intercepted enciphered messages. For example, as Morse noted in developing the assignments of dots and dashes to characters in the English language, the letter E is the most frequently occurring character, followed by the letter T. Thus, Morse assigned a dot to denote E and a dash to denote T prior to assigning sequences of dots and dashes to denote other characters in his code.

Suppose, for example, that you intercept a message enciphered using the plaintext-ciphertext relationship illustrated in Table 3.2. Further assume that you perform a frequency

analysis of the characters in the enciphered message and discover that the letter M occurs most frequently, followed by the character S. In this case, your first attempt to reconstruct the plaintext-ciphertext alphabet relationship in order to decipher the message would result in placing the character E in the plaintext alphabet over the character M in the ciphertext alphabet, followed by placing the character T in the plaintext alphabet over the character S in the ciphertext alphabet. Although a frequency analysis may not provide an exact relationship between plaintext and ciphertext characters, the analysis normally provides enough intelligent clues to conduct a successful decipherment if you gain access to one long message or a few short messages enciphered using the same alphabetic relationship.

★ TOP ★
SECRET

4

TRANSPOSITION-BASED MONOALPHABETIC SUBSTITUTION

This chapter focuses on three commonly used methods to develop a mixed alphabet. The first two methods are related to the use of arrays or matrices, and the third method can be considered a position-and-extraction technique. After you obtain an understanding of the manual process required for the formation of a transposition mixed alphabet and the encipherment of a message using that alphabet, I'll turn your attention to automation. I'll show you how to develop a series of subroutines that you can use to perform different types of transpositions and how to incorporate these subroutines into a program. When possible, existing subroutines are employed to take advantage of your previous efforts.

MATRIX-BASED TRANSPOSITION

By placing an alphabet into an *n x n* matrix or array you can obtain the ability to extract characters in many different ways. For example, consider the sequential plaintext alphabet placed into a *7 x 4* matrix (see Figure 4.1). Each character in the alphabet is referenced by a row and column position and can be considered an element in the array or matrix. By extracting matrix elements in a predefined sequence, you can develop a transposed alphabet.

Figure 4.1.
The placement of a plaintext alphabet into a matrix. Each character in the matrix is identified by its row and column position.

COLUMNS

	1	2	3	4	5	6	7
1	A	B	C	D	E	F	G
2	H	I	J	K	L	M	N
3	O	P	Q	R	S	T	U
4	V	W	X	Y	Z		

ROWS

Perhaps the earliest use of a matrix with a cryptographic alphabet can be traced to the Greek writer Polybius. He arranged the Greek alphabet into a square and numbered the rows and columns whose values identified the location of each letter. This enabled each letter to be identified by a pair of numbers that represented the intersection of a row and column in the matrix.

In addition to devising the use of a matrix for cryptographic applications, Polybius suggested the use of his matrix as a mechanism to transmit information by torches. Polybius proposed that letters in the alphabet could be transmitted over relatively long distances by persons holding a different number of torches. For example, a person holding one torch at his right and two to his left would signal the letter located at the intersection of the first row and second column in the matrix.

> *The formation of an alphabet into a matrix was rediscovered by modern cryptographers and formed the basis for the development of a large number of encipherment systems. Some systems convert letters into numbers, and other systems use the matrix to form different types of alphabets based on the extraction of row and column entries using a predefined algorithm.*

If you extract the matrix elements in each column, commencing with column seven working backward, extracting the elements in column six, column five, and so on, the transposed alphabet GNUFMTELSZDKRYCJQXBIPWAHOV is created. If you extract the matrix elements in a progressive column order, the transposed alphabet AHOVBIPWCJQXDKRYELSZFMTGNU is produced.

Unfortunately, the placement of a plaintext alphabet into a matrix produces a transposed alphabet in which several sequences of letters are displaced by fixed positions—making the job of a cryptanalyst easier if she or he attempts to reconstruct the transposed alphabet used to encipher messages. To add a degree of difficulty to any reconstruction attempt, these alphabets are normally developed through the use of a keyword or keyword phrase.

Figure 4.2 illustrates the construction of a keyword-based, mixed alphabet fitted into a *7 x 4* matrix, using KEYWORD as the keyword. Similar to the keyword-based alphabets discussed in Chapter 3, "Keyword-Based Monoalphabetic Substitution," you can use either a keyword or keyword phrase to develop a mixed alphabet. By placing the resulting alphabet into a matrix, you can develop a transposed keyword-based, mixed alphabet. The construction of this alphabet is easy to duplicate, and it provides the message recipient with an easy mechanism for preparing to decipher a received message. In addition, using a keyword or keyword phrase adds an additional degree of difficulty to a cryptanalyst attempting to decipher a message that intentionally or unintentionally falls into his or her hands.

Figure 4.2.
*A keyword-
based, mixed
alphabet placed
into a matrix. In
this example,
the keyword
KEYWORD was
used to form the
keyword-based,
mixed alphabet.*

```
                    COLUMNS

              1   2   3   4   5   6   7

          1   K   E   Y   W   O   R   D

          2   A   B   C   F   G   H   I
   ROWS
          3   J   L   M   N   P   Q   S

          4   T   U   V   X   Z
```

Note in Figure 4.2 that the keyword used is seven positions in length and defines the number of columns in the matrix. When developing a keyword-based, mixed alphabet, remember to remove any duplicate letters in the keyword or keyword phrase and add the remaining letters of the alphabet (those not contained in the keyword or keyword phrase) in the sequence in which they appear in the alphabet. The keyword ALPHA, for example, would be reduced to ALPH to eliminate the duplicate A. (This would also create a four-column matrix.)

SIMPLE TRANSPOSITION

There are several methods that can be used to develop a transposed keyword-based, mixed alphabet. Perhaps the most obvious method, referred to as *simple transposition*, extracts column entries in their column order. The simple transposition of the keyword-based alphabet illustrated in Figure 4.2 produces the following keyword-based simple transposed alphabet:

KAJTEBLUYCMVWFNXOGPZRHQDIS

After you create the transposed alphabet, you can use it for the plaintext or the ciphertext alphabet. You can also create two different transposed alphabets and use one for the plaintext alphabet and the second for the ciphertext alphabet. (The examples presented in this chapter restrict the use of transposed alphabets to the ciphertext alphabet.)

ENCIPHERMENT

Similar to previously described manual encipherment processes, you should list the plaintext alphabet above the ciphertext alphabet. For each character in the plaintext message, locate that character in the plaintext alphabet and extract the corresponding character by position in the ciphertext alphabet. Figure 4.3 illustrates the encipherment of the first two characters of a plaintext message using the previously developed keyword-based simple transposed alphabet.

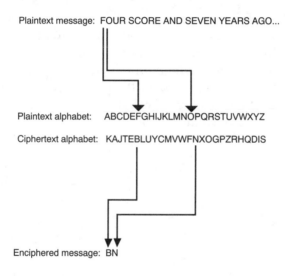

Figure 4.3.
Encipherment using a keyword-based simple transposed alphabet.

DECIPHERMENT

The decipherment process can be considered as the reverse of the previously illustrated encipherment process—rearrange your sheet of paper to place the enciphered message at the top of the page and list the ciphertext alphabet above the plaintext alphabet. Then take each character in the enciphered message and locate it in the ciphertext alphabet, extracting the plaintext alphabet character in the equivalent position of the ciphertext character in the ciphertext alphabet.

NUMERIC KEYED TRANSPOSITION

Another popular method used to develop a transposed alphabet through the use of a matrix involves the selection of rows based on the alphabetic position of the character in the keyword. This technique is known as *numeric transposition* because a numeric is normally assigned to each column based on the location of the first character in the column relative to the characters in the adjusted keyword. The characters in each column are then extracted to form the transposed alphabet based on the numeric value assigned to each column.

Figure 4.4 illustrates the construction of a numeric transposition-based alphabet using the keyword KEYWORD. Note that a numeric is assigned to each column based on the position of the first character in each column in the first row of characters. Simply extract the characters in each column based on the numeric sequence of each column.

Figure 4.4.
Constructing a numeric transposition-based alphabet.

COLUMNS

	3	2	7	6	4	5	1
1	K	E	Y	W	O	R	D
2	A	B	C	F	G	H	I
3	J	L	M	N	P	Q	S
4	T	U	V	X	Z		

ROWS

Resulting alphabet:

DISEBLUKAJTOGPZRHQWFNZYCMV

ENCIPHERMENT AND DECIPHERMENT

After you create a numeric-based transposition alphabet, you can use that alphabet as the ciphertext alphabet. You can then encipher and decipher messages in the same manner as previously described for the simple transposition alphabet.

OTHER VARIATIONS

Once a keyword- or keyword phrase-based alphabet is placed into a matrix, you can use several additional extraction techniques to form a transposition alphabet. Other variations you can consider include reversed simple and reversed numeric transpositions as well as different diagonally formed transpositions. Because the simple and conventional numeric transpositions are the primary methods used for the formation of transposed alphabets, I'll leave it as an exercise for you to develop other types of transposed alphabets.

The use of a matrix for enciphering messages provides a mechanism for supplementing or circumventing the use of more secure systems. During World War II, General Leslie Groves, who was in charge of the Manhattan Project, needed a mechanism to discuss secret matters over the telephone. General Groves developed a series of 10 x 10 matrices in which each matrix contained both letters of the alphabet and code-word characters that represented different laboratory or manufacturing sites.

To reduce the possibility of an analysis of an overheard telephone conversation, General Groves took two actions. First, he developed a different matrix for each person he needed to talk to concerning matters of national security. This reduced the potential effect of the loss of a matrix and made it more difficult for a series of overheard conversations to be analyzed. Within each matrix, General Groves also located multiple copies of frequently occurring letters in the English language, such as the letters A, E, I, O, U, and T. The number of repetitions of a character depended upon the frequency of occurrence of the letter in the alphabet. For example, in one of the general's matrices, he included nine Es and seven Ts. This technique considerably reduced the possibility and effectiveness of frequency analysis.

INTERVAL EXTRACTION

The last technique discussed in this chapter that is used to create a program to automate its operation involves the extraction of characters from the plaintext alphabet based on a predefined interval. As each letter in the alphabet is extracted, it is removed from the plaintext alphabet and entered into the interval extracted alphabet.

Listing 4.1 illustrates two examples of the formation of interval extracted alphabets based on the use of an interval of three positions. In the example in the top portion of Listing 4.1, the interval 3 extraction process is applied against a sequential plaintext alphabet. In the example in the bottom portion of Listing 4.1, the interval 3 extraction process is applied against a keyword-based, mixed alphabet using KEYWORD as the keyword. Note the significant differences between the resulting extracted alphabets even though the extraction interval was the same for each example.

Listing 4.1 Developing interval extracted alphabets.

```
               Interval 3 extraction of plaintext alphabet
Plaintext alphabet:                         ABCDEFGHIJKLMNOPQRSTUVWXYZ
Resulting interval 3 extracted alphabet:    CFILORUXAEJNSWBHPVDMYKZTGQ


               Interval 3 extraction of keyword-based, mixed alphabet
Keyword-based, mixed alphabet:              KEYWORDABCFGHIJLMNPQSTUVXZ
Resulting interval 3 extracted alphabet:    YRBGJNSVKOCIPUEALTWHXFZQDM
```

ENCIPHERMENT AND DECIPHERMENT

Once an interval extracted alphabet is formed, it can be used in the same manner as the simple and numeric-based transposition alphabets. You can use the interval 3 extracted alphabet in Listing 4.1 as the ciphertext alphabet for enciphering a message as previously illustrated in Figure 4.3. Similarly, you can use that alphabet and its relationship to the plaintext alphabet to decipher an enciphered message.

AUTOMATING MATRIX-BASED SYSTEMS

To facilitate the automation process required to encipher messages based on transposition-based mixed alphabets, you can create two new subroutines. One subroutine, which I'll label TRANSPORT, can be used to form either a simple or a numeric transposition mixed alphabet sequence based on the user's preference. The second subroutine, which I'll label INTERVAL, can be used to create an extracted alphabet based on a pre-defined interval or position. After you create these two subroutines, you can add them to the existing CIPHER5.BAS program and change the main portion of the program to permit the newly created subroutines to be invoked. The resulting program, which I'll call CIPHER6.BAS, permits users to dynamically enter the name of the files they wish to use to store an input plaintext message and the resulting enciphered message.

THE SUBROUTINE TRANSPORT

Listing 4.2 contains the contents of the subroutine labeled TRANSPORT, which creates either a simple or numeric transposition mixed-sequence alphabet. This subroutine includes several unnecessary PRINT statements to illustrate how the program operates. Similar to the previous use of extraneous PRINT statements, I have identified those statements with comments consisting of five asterisks to facilitate their removal.

Listing 4.2. The TRANSPORT subroutine.

```
TRANSPORT:
        REM Routine to form simple or numeric transposition-
        ➥mixed sequence
        REM Initialize 26 by 26 matrix to nulls
                POSITION = 0
                FOR I = 0 TO 26
                FOR J = 0 16
                TRANS$(I, J) = ""
                NEXT J, I
```

continues

Listing 4.2. Continued

```
          REM Determine actual matrix size
                  COLUMN = LEN(KEYCOL$)
                  ROW = 26 / COLUMN - INT(26 / COLUMN)
                  IF ROW > 0 THEN ROW = (INT(26 / COLUMN) + 1)
                    ELSE ROW = 26 / COLUMN
          REM Place keyword-based alphabet into matrix elements
                  PRINT "MATRIX IS:" PRINT
                  FOR I = 0 TO ROW - 1
                  FOR J = 0 TO COLUMN - 1
                  IF POSITION > 25 THEN GOTO ALLDONE
                  TRANS$(I, J) = PLAINTEXT$(POSITION)
                  PRINT TRANS$(I, J)                          '*****
                  POSITION = POSITION + 1
                  NEXT J
                  PRINT                                       '*****
ALLDONE:          NEXT I
                  PRINT : PRINT
          IF ORDER$ = "NUMERIC" GOTO NUMERIC
          REM Form simple transposition-based mixed alphabet
                  X$ = ""
                  FOR I = 0 TO COLUMN - 1
                  FOR J = 0 TO ROW - 1
                  X$ = X$ + LTRIM$(TRANS$(J, I))
                  NEXT J
                  NEXT I
          REM Place into PLAINTEXT array
                  FOR I = 0 TO 25
                  PLAINTEXT$(I) = MID$(X$, I + 1, 1)
                  NEXT I
          RETURN
          REM Form numeric transposition-based mixed alphabet
NUMERIC:          FOR I = 0 TO COLUMN - 1
                  TEMP$(I) = TRANS$(0, I)'place in temporary
➥storage first row
                  NEXT I
```

```
                FOR I = 0 TO COLUMN - 1'begin sort
                FOR J = I + 1 TO COLUMN - 1
                IF TEMP$(I) > TEMP$(J) THEN SWAP TEMP$(I),
➥TEMP$(J)
                NEXT J
                NEXT I 'TEMP$ array now contains sorted order
➥of characters
            REM Compare sorted keyword to first column in matrix,
➥extract
            REM when they match by getting row contents
                X$ = " "
                FOR I = 0 TO COLUMN - 1'
                FOR J = 0 TO COLUMN - 1
                IF TEMP$(I) <> TRANS$(O, J) GOTO NMATCH
                FOR K = 0 TO ROW - 1        'match, get row
➥contents
                X$ = X$ + LTRIM$(TRANS$(K, J))
                NEXT K
NMATCH:         NEXT J
                NEXT I
            REM Place into PLAINTEXT array
                FOR I = 0 TO 25
                PLAINTEXT$(I) = MID$(X$, I + 1, 1)
                NEXT I
RETURN
```

The first group of statements in the subroutine TRANSPORT initializes a *26 x 26* string matrix labeled TRANS$ to nulls. This matrix permits a keyword or keyword phrase that can be up to 26 characters in length. The second group of statements determines the actual size of the matrix. Here, the value of COLUMN is the length of the keyword in characters. A keyword consisting of five characters requires a matrix of five columns and six rows for all 26 letters of the alphabet to fit into the matrix.

The third group of statements places the characters of a keyword-based alphabet into the string array TRANS$. Note that the values of the indices of the nested FOR-NEXT loops are

adjusted by subtracting 1 from the values of ROW and COLUMN because the matrix elements commence at position 0,0. Also note that values are assigned to TRANS$ from the string array PLAINTEXT$. The array PLAINTEXT$ contains the keyword-developed alphabet, which was filled by the prior invoking of the previously described KEYWORD subroutine. Therefore, you must invoke KEYWORD before you invoke TRANSPORT. To facilitate passing information to determine the number of columns in the matrix, the statement KEYCOL$=X$ was added to the end of the third group of statements in the KEYWORD subroutine.

The PRINT statements included in the third group of statements simply display the matrix for your review (they are removed from the subroutine later in this chapter). The IF statement permits the selection of a simple or numeric-based mixed alphabet. If the string variable ORDER$ does not equal NUMERIC, the simple transposition-based mixed alphabet is formed. This occurs in the fourth statement group, which simply adds each character in every row of each column to the string X$ in column sequence. The resulting simple transposition-based mixed alphabet is placed into the string array PLAINTEXT$ and the subroutine ends.

If the user wants a numeric transposition-based mixed alphabet, a branch to the label NUMERIC in the subroutine occurs. At this location, the first character in each column is placed into temporary storage in the string array TEMP$. The contents of TEMP$ are then sorted—the array contains the characters of the keyword in sorted order. This is followed by another group of statements that cycle through the elements of the TEMP$ array. Each element of that array is matched against the first character in each column of the TRANS$ array. When a match occurs, the contents of the column are extracted and added to the string X$, which results in the formation of a numeric transposition mixed-sequence alphabet. The last group of statements places the resulting alphabet into the string array PLAINTEXT$.

Listing 4.3 illustrates the modified calling sequence used to invoke the subroutine TRANSPORT. This calling sequence displays the formed matrix, ciphertext alphabet, and plaintext alphabet to enable you to verify the operation of the subroutine. To enable you to use the calling sequence and the TRANSPORT subroutine, the code has been stored in a file labeled CIPHERTR.BAS on the convenience disk. (The PRINT statements that display the matrix and alphabets will be removed when you develop the program CIPHER6.BAS.)

Listing 4.3. The main part of CIPHERTR.BAS and the calling sequence to invoke TRANSPORT subroutine.

```
REM PROGRAM CIPHERTR.BAS
DIM PLAINTEXT$(26), CIPHERTEXT$(26), KEY$(26), TRANS$(26, 26),
➡TEMP$(26)
        CLS
        PRINT "PROGRAM CIPHERTR.BAS enciphers a message using a
        ➡transposition matrix"
        PRINT "and a monoalphabetic substitution process based
        ➡upon a keyword "
        PRINT "or keyword phrase and an alphabetic shift key."
        PRINT
GOSUB INITIALIZE
        INPUT "Enter keyword or keyword phrase in UPPERCASE: ",
        ➡TEXT$
        PRINT "Plaintext based alphabet is : "; '*****
        FOR I = 0 TO 25: PRINT PLAINTEXT$(I); : NEXT I '*****
GOSUB KEYWORD                    'form keyword-based, mixed alphabet
        PRINT "Keyword-based alphabet is : "; X$  '*****
        INPUT "Enter transposition matrix method - SIMPLE or
        ➡NUMERIC :", ORDER$
GOSUB TRANSPORT
        PRINT ORDER$; " Transposition Alphabet is :"; X$
1       INPUT "Enter UPPERCASE Alphabetic Shift Key: ", K$
        FOR I = 0 TO 25
        IF K$ = PLAINTEXT$(I) GOTO 2
```

continues

Listing 4.3. Continued

```
        NEXT I
        PRINT "You must enter a letter from A to Z"
        GOTO 1
2       REM Position I represents shift key letter

GOSUB FORMCIPHER              'create cipher alphabet
        PRINT "Shifted keyword mixed alphabet is : "; '*****
        FOR I = 0 TO 25: PRINT CIPHERTEXT$(I); : NEXT I: PRINT
        ➥'*****
GOSUB INITIALIZE              'reinitialize plaintext array
GOSUB MSGFILE                 'assign I/O files, place message on
                              ➥a file
GOSUB CONVERTSTORE            'convert and store ciphertext on a
                              ➥file
GOSUB PRTOUT                  'print results
END
```

THE CIPHERTR.BAS PROGRAM

Listing 4.4 illustrates the execution of the program CIPHERTR.BAS to encipher a message based on the use of a simple transposition mixed-sequence alphabet and an alphabetic shift key. This example uses the keyword KEYWORD and the alphabetic shift character C. Note the display of the 4-row-by-7-column matrix formed by the TRANSPORT subroutine. Because a SIMPLE transposition method was selected, the letters in the matrix are extracted in column order, KAJT followed by EBLU, and so on. This is verified by the line after the end of the matrix display.

Listing 4.4. The execution of CIPHERTR.BAS program using a simple transposition keyword mixed alphabet.

```
PROGRAM CIPHERTR.BAS enciphers a message using a transposition
➥matrix
and a monoalphabetic substitution process based on a keyword
or keyword phrase and an alphabetic shift key.
```

```
Enter keyword or keyword phrase in UPPERCASE: KEYWORD
Plaintext-based alphabet is : ABCDEFGHIJKLMNOPQRSTUVWXYZ
Keyword-based alphabet is : KEYWORDABCFGHIJLMNPQSTUVXZ
Enter transposition matrix method - SIMPLE OR NUMERIC: SIMPLE
MATRIX IS:


KEYWORD
ABCFGHI
JLMNPQS
TUVXZ


SIMPLE Transposition Alphabet is : KAJTEBLUYCMVWFNXOGPZRHQDIS
Enter UPPERCASE Alphabetic Shift Key: C
Shifted keyword mixed alphabet is : MVWFNXOGPZRHQDISKAJTEBLUYC
Enter filename to store plaintext message, default=MESSAGE.DAT
Enter filename to store enciphered message, default=CIPHERTX.DAT
Select keyboard (k) or file (f) message input: K
enter your message - place a / at the beginning of each line
that should remain in plaintext and a \ on a separate line
to indicate the end of the enciphered message

/TO BILL
/FROM AL
MEET ME IN ST LOUIS ON FRIDAY FEBRUARY
THIRTEEN AT NINE PM
\
Press Return key to display resulting enciphered message




Resulting enciphered message is:
TO BILL
FROM AL
QNNTQ NPDJT HIEPJ IDXAP FMYXN
VAEMA YTGPA TNNDM TDPDN SQXXX
```

As in previous examples, an alphabetic shift key character results in the shift of a previously developed alphabet so that the position of the shift key letter is rotated to the right of the

alphabet. Entering the shift key C rotates the simple transposition alphabet by ten positions.

The plaintext alphabet should be compared to the shifted-keyword mixed alphabet for the encipherment of a message because the latter alphabet is the ciphertext alphabet. In this example, the message to be enciphered is MEET ME IN ST LOUIS ON FRIDAY FEBRUARY THIRTEEN AT NINE PM. The M in the plaintext alphabet corresponds to the letter Q in the shifted-keyword mixed alphabet. Thus, the first character in the enciphered message is Q. The character E in the message is located in the plaintext alphabet. Because its position corresponds to the position of the character N in the shifted-keyword mixed alphabet, replace E by N and continue the process to verify the operation of the portion of the program that enciphers a message based on a simple transposition mixed alphabet and an alphabetic shift key.

Listing 4.5 illustrates the execution of the program CIPERTR.BAS when a numeric transposition mixed alphabet is selected. Because D is the lowest character in the keyword KEYWORD, the characters in the column headed by D are extracted first. Thus, DIS are the first three letters displayed for the numeric transposition alphabet. Because E is the next lowest letter in the keyword, the contents of the column headed by E are added to the alphabet—EBLU follows the characters DIS. You can examine the remainder of Listing 4.5 to verify that the message is enciphered correctly by using the relationship between the plaintext and shifted-keyword mixed alphabets.

Listing 4.5. The execution of CIPHERTR.BAS program using a numeric transposition matrix keyword mixed alphabet.

```
PROGRAM CIPHERTR.BAS enciphers a message using a transposition
➡matrix
and a monoalphabetic substitution process based on a keyword
or keyword phrase and an alphabetic shift key.
```

```
Enter keyword or keyword phrase in UPPERCASE: KEYWORD
Plaintext-based alphabet is : ABCDEFGHIJKLMNOPQRSTUVWXYZ
Keyword-based alphabet is : KEYWORDABCFGHIJLMNPQSTUVXZ
Enter transposition matrix method - SIMPLE OR NUMERIC: NUMERIC
MATRIX IS:

KEYWORD
ABCFGHI
JLMNPQS
TUVXZ


NUMERIC Transposition Alphabet is : DISEBLUKAJTOGPZRHQWFNXYCMV
Enter UPPERCASE Alphabetic Shift Key: C
Shifted keyword mixed alphabet is : MVDISEBLUKAJTOGPZRHQWFNXYC
Enter filename to store plaintext message, default=MESSAGE.DAT
Enter filename to store enciphered message, default=CIPHERTX.DAT
Select keyboard (k) or file (f) message input: K
Enter your message - place a / at the beginning of each line
that should remain in plaintext and a \ on a separate line
to indicate the end of the enciphered message

/TO BILL
/FROM AL
MEET ME IN ST LOUIS ON FRIDAY FEBRUARY
THIRTEEN AT NINE PM
\
Press Return key to display resulting enciphered message




Resulting enciphered message is:
TO BILL
FROM AL
TSSQT SUOHQ JGWUH GOERU IMYES
VRWMR YQLUR QSSOM QOUOS PTXX
```

INTERVAL EXTRACTION ROUTINE

Listing 4.6 contains the contents of the subroutine INTERVAL, which forms an interval extracted alphabet based on a pre-defined interval that is passed to the subroutine in the variable INTERVAL.

Listing 4.6. The subroutine INTERVAL.

```
INTERVAL:
        REM Subroutine to form interval extracted alphabet
        COUNT = 0
        I = INTERVAL - 1  'adjust since array starts at 0
        X$ = ""
        DO UNTIL COUNT >= 26
                X$ = X$ + PLAINTEXT$(I)
                COUNT = COUNT + 1
                I = I + INTERVAL
                IF I >= 26 THEN I = I - 26
        LOOP
        REM Put back into PLAINTEXT$ array
        FOR I = 0 TO 25
        PLAINTEXT$(I) = MID$(X$, I + 1, 1)
        NEXT I
RETURN
```

Note in Listing 4.6 that the interval value is decreased by 1 because the array starts at element 0. The DO UNTIL COUNT loop extracts each character from the string array PLAINTEXT$ until all the characters are extracted. Note that whenever I equals or exceeds 26, you should reset I to I-26, which recirculates the sequence. Also note that because you are using the string array PLAINTEXT$, you must invoke the subroutine KEYWORD before you invoke the subroutine INTERVAL if you wish to use an interval extraction based on a keyword mixed alphabet. Similar to the TRANSPORT subroutine, conclude the INTERVAL subroutine by placing the interval extracted alphabet back into the array PLAINTEXT$.

THE CIPHER6.BAS PROGRAM

To illustrate the execution of the interval extraction subroutine, I'll incorporate that routine into a program that enciphers messages based on any one of the three alphabet formation techniques presented earlier in this chapter: interval extraction, simple transposition, and numeric transposition. This program, CIPHER6.BAS on the convenience disk, contains extraneous PRINT statements highlighted with five asterisks as comments (included to explain the operation of the program). You may want to remove these statements from the program if you wish to use it or distribute it to associates.

Listing 4.7 contains the statements that make up the main portion of the CIPHER6.BAS program. The first group of statements starting with the label START simply displays the program's options, accepts the user-specified enciphering method, and assigns a value to the string variable ORDER$ based on the type of enciphering technique selected.

Listing 4.7. The main portion of CIPHER6.BAS program.

```
REM PROGRAM CIPHER6.BAS
DIM PLAINTEXT$(26), CIPHERTEXT$(26), KEY$(26), TRANS$(26, 26),
➥TEMP$(26)
START:  CLS
        PRINT "Program CIPHER6.BAS enciphers a message using
        ➥one"
        PRINT "of the following technigues to form a cipher
        ➥alphabet"
        PRINT " (1) Interval Extraction Sequence"
        PRINT " (2) Simple Transposition Sequence"
        PRINT " (3) Numeric Transposition Sequence"
        PRINT
        INPUT "Enter method to form enciphered message 1, 2 or
        ➥3: ", X
        IF X < 1 OR X > 3 THEN GOTO START
        IF X = 2 THEN ORDER$ = "SIMPLE"
        IF X = 3 THEN ORDER$ = "NUMERIC"
        IF X > 1 THEN GOTO TRAN
```

continues

Listing 4.7. Continued

```
        INPUT "Enter the interval as a number between 1 and 25:
        ➥", INTERVAL
TRAN:   INPUT "Enter keyword or keyword phrase in UPPERCASE: ",
        ➥TEXT$
        PRINT
GOSUB INITIALIZE
        PRINT "Plaintext based alphabet is : "; '*****
        FOR I = 0 TO 25: PRINT PLAINTEXT$(I); : NEXT I   '*****
GOSUB KEYWORD                    'form keyword based mixed alphabet
        PRINT "Keyword based alphabet is : "; X$ '*****
ON X GOSUB INTERVAL, TRANSPORT, TRANSPORT
        IF X = 1 THEN PRINT "Interval Alphabet is : "; X$
        IF X > 1 THEN PRINT ORDER$; " Transposition Alphabet is
        ➥:"; X$
1       INPUT "Enter UPPERCASE Alphabetic Shift Key: ", K$
        FOR I = 0 TO 25
        IF K$ = PLAINTEXT$(I) GOTO 2
        NEXT I
        PRINT "You must enter a letter from A to Z"
        GOTO 1
2       REM Position I represents shift key letter

GOSUB FORMCIPHER                 'create cipher alphabet
        PRINT "Shifted keyword mixed alphabet is : "; '*****
        FOR I = 0 TO 25: PRINT CIPHERTEXT$(I); : NEXT I: PRINT
        ➥'*****
GOSUB INITIALIZE                 'reinitialize plaintext array
GOSUB MSGFILE                    'assign I/O files, place message on
                                    ➥a file
GOSUB CONVERTSTORE               'convert and store ciphertext on a
                                    ➥file
GOSUB PRTOUT                     'print results
END
```

If an interval extraction technique is selected, the user is prompted to enter the interval to be used. Regardless of the enciphering method selected, the user is prompted to enter a keyword or keyword phrase used to form a keyword-based, mixed alphabet. Both the plaintext alphabet and keyword-based, mixed alphabet are displayed through the use of extraneous PRINT statements that you can remove. You should note that the subroutines INITIALIZE and KEYWORD, as well as the other subroutines invoked from the main portion of CIPHER6.BAS, contain the statements previously described in this book and will not be reviewed again.

The ON X GOSUB statement causes a branch to the INTERVAL or TRANSPORT subroutine based on the user-selected encipherment method assigned to the variable X. After one of these subroutines is invoked, the appropriate alphabet is displayed by the use of extraneous IF-THEN PRINT statements that can be removed from the program. The program then accepts an alphabetic shift key, invokes the FORMCIPHER subroutine, and displays the shifted keyword mixed alphabet which, in effect, is the cipher alphabet. Again, you can remove the extraneous PRINT statements if you so desire. Thereafter, the program invokes four more subroutines that reinitialize the plaintext array, assign I/O files and place a message on a file, convert and store the ciphertext on a file, and print the results of the encipherment operation.

Listing 4.8 illustrates the execution of CIPHER6.BAS when an interval extraction technique is used to form a cipher alphabet. In this example, the keyword MICROSOFT was used to form the keyword-based alphabet. It is this alphabet that is used as the basis for forming the interval alphabet. Because 3 was entered as the extraction interval, every third character in the keyword-based alphabet is removed to form the interval alphabet. Thus, C is extracted, followed by S, and so on from the keyword-based alphabet.

 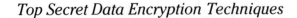

Listing 4.8. The execution of CIPHER6.BAS.

```
PROGRAM CIPHER6.BAS ENCIPHERS A MESSAGE USING ONE
OF THE FOLLOWING TECHNIQUES TO FORM A CIPHER ALPHABET
    (1)  INTERVAL EXTRACTION SEQUENCE
    (2)  SIMPLE TRANSPOSITION SEQUENCE
    (3)  NUMERIC TRANSPOSITION SEQUENCE


Enter method to form enciphered message 1, 2, or 3: 1
Enter the interval as a numeric between 1 and 25: 3
Enter keyword or keyword phrase in UPPERCASE: MICROSOFT


Plaintext-based alphabet is : ABCDEFGHIJKLMNOPQRSTUVWXYZ
Keyword-based alphabet is : MICROSFTABDEGHJKLNPQUVWXYZ
Interval alphabet is : CSAEJNUXMRFBGKPVYIOTDHLQWZ
Enter UPPERCASE Alphabetic Shift Key: B
Shifted keyword mixed alphabet is : GKPVYIOTDHLQWZCSAEJNUXMRFB
Enter filename to store plaintext message, default=MESSAGE.DAT
Enter filename to store enciphered message, default=CIPHERTX.DAT
Select keyboard (k) or file (f) message input: K
Enter your message - place a / at the beginning of each line
that should remain in plaintext and a \ on a separate line
to indicate the end of the enciphered message


/TO DAN
/FROM GEORGE
WE MUST MEET QUICKLY TO DISCUSS THE USE
OF THE ENGLISH LANGUAGE AND SPELLING OF
COMMONLY USED FOODE
\
Press Return key to display resulting enciphered message




Resulting enciphered message is:
TO DAN
FROM GEORGE
```

```
MYWUJ NWYYN AUDPL QFNCV DJPUJ
JNTYU JYCIN TYYZO QDJTQ GZOUG
OYGZV JSYQQ DZOCI PCWWC ZQFUJ
YVICC VYXXX
```

The selection of B as the shift key causes the interval alphabet to be rotated so that the character B in the alphabet is positioned at the extreme right. The resulting shifted-keyword mixed alphabet formed using an interval extraction method represents the ciphertext alphabet. Thus, first locate each character in the message in the plaintext alphabet and extract the character in the equivalent position in the shifted-keyword mixed alphabet.

Note that the message WE MUST MEET results in the enciphered message MYMUJ NWYYN. You can verify the accuracy of the encipherment process by noting that the position of W in the plaintext message is equivalent to M in the shifted-keyword mixed alphabet, E has the same position as Y, and so on.

DECIPHERMENT

You can easily construct a program to decipher messages previously enciphered through the use of an interval extraction, simple transposition, or a numeric transposition sequence used to form a cipher alphabet. In doing so, you can use the subroutines contained in the DCIPHER5.BAS program, change the main portion of the program to reflect the selection of one of the three decipherment techniques under consideration, and add the subroutines INTERVAL and TRANSPORT. The resulting program, contained in the file DCIPHER6.BAS on the convenience disk, is named as such because it should be used to decipher messages previously enciphered through the CIPHER6.BAS program.

THE DCIPHER6.BAS PROGRAM

Listing 4.9 contains the statements in the main program of the DCIPHER6.BAS program. You should note that the main portion of DCIPHER6.BAS is almost an exact duplicate of CIPHER6.BAS (the differences between these programs relate to the use of the term *decipher* in place of *encipher* and the inclusion of the subroutines DMSGFILE and DCONVERTSTORE in place of MSGFILE and CONVERTSTORE). As explained previously, the prefix D on a subroutine is used to indicate a modification to a previously developed subroutine—a deciphering operation in place of an enciphering operation. Similar to other programs in this chapter, a comment consisting of five asterisks is used to indicate an extraneous PRINT statement included for explanation purposes (these statements can be removed from the program).

Listing 4.9. The main portion of DCIPHER6.BAS program.

```
REM PROGRAM CIPHER6.BAS
DIM PLAINTEXT$(26), CIPHERTEXT$(26), KEY$(26), TRANS$(26, 26),
➡TEMP$(26)
START:  CLS
        PRINT "PROGRAM DCIPHER6.BAS DECIPHERS A MESSAGE USING
        ➡ONE"
        PRINT "OF THE FOLLOWING TECHNIQUES TO FORM A CIPHER
        ➡ALPHABET"
        PRINT " (1) INTERVAL EXTRACTION SEQUENCE"
        PRINT " (2) SIMPLE TRANSPOSITION SEQUENCE"
        PRINT " (3) NUMERIC TRANSPOSITION SEQUENCE"
        PRINT
        INPUT "Enter method to be used to decipher a message 1,
        ➡2 or 3: ", X
        IF X < 1 OR X > 3 THEN GOTO START
        IF X = 2 THEN ORDER$ = "SIMPLE"
        IF X = 3 THEN ORDER$ = "NUMERIC"
        IF X > 1 THEN GOTO TRAN
        INPUT "Enter the interval as a numeric between 1 and 25:
        ➡", INTERVAL
TRAN:   INPUT "Enter keyword or keyword phrase in UPPERCASE: ",
        ➡TEXT$
```

```
        PRINT
GOSUB INITIALIZE
        PRINT "Plaintext based alphabet is : "; '*****
        FOR I = 0 TO 25: PRINT PLAINTEXT$(I); : NEXT I  '*****
GOSUB KEYWORD                   'form keyword-based, mixed alphabet
        PRINT "Keyword based alphabet is : "; X$ '*****
ON X GOSUB INTERVAL, TRANSPORT, TRANSPORT
        IF X = 1 THEN PRINT "Interval Alphabet is : "; X$
        IF X > 1 THEN PRINT ORDER$; "Transposition Alphabet is
        ➡:"; X$
1       INPUT "Enter UPPERCASE Alphabetic Shift Key: ", K$
        FOR I = 0 TO 25
        IF K$ = PLAINTEXT$(I) GOTO 2
        NEXT I
        PRINT "You must enter a letter from A to Z"
        GOTO 1
2       REM Position I represents shift key letter

GOSUB FORMCIPHER                'create cipher alphabet
        PRINT "Shifted keyword mixed alphabet is : "; '*****
        FOR I = 0 TO 25: PRINT CIPHERTEXT$(I); : NEXT I: PRINT
        ➡'*****
GOSUB INITIALIZE                'reinitialize plaintext array
GOSUB DMSGFILE                  'assign I/O files, place message
                                ➡on a file
GOSUB DCONVERTSTORE             'convert and store ciphertext on a
                                ➡file
GOSUB PRTOUT                    'print results
END
```

To illustrate the use of DCIPHER6.BAS, first execute
CIPHER6.BAS. Listing 4.10 illustrates the plaintext message and
its resulting enciphered message when an interval extraction
sequence of 3, the keyword MAYDECEMBER, and the alphabetic shift
key (B) are used to form the shifted-keyword mixed alphabet.

Listing 4.10. Enciphering a sample message using the CIPHER6.BAS program.

```
/TO FIDEL
/FROM GORBY
PLEASE NOTE THAT A FEW CHANGES IN THE EAST
NOW WARRANT YOUR CONSIDERATION OF CHANGING
CUBAN ECONOMY TO THE CAPITALISTIC SYSTEM STOP
OTHERWISE REMEMBER FAMOUS FATE OF ROMANIAN LEADER
STOP BEST REGARDS STOP
\
Press Return key to display the resulting enciphered message



    Resulting enciphered message is
    TO FIDEL
    FROM GORBY
    YOUGI UVZLU LEGLG XUWNE GVAUI
    RVLEU UGILV ZWWGF FGVLD ZPFNZ
    VIRQU FGLRZ VZXNE GVARV ANPJG
    VUNZV ZSDLZ LEUNG YRLGO RILRN
    IDILU SILZY ZLEUF WRIUF USUSJ
    UFXGS ZPIXG LUZXF ZSGVR GVOUG
    QUFIL ZYJUI LFUAG FQIIL ZYXXX
```

Listing 4.11 illustrates the use of the DCIPHER6.BAS program to decipher the previously enciphered message. Note that the message recipient must know the type of technique used to encipher the message, the keyword or keyword phrase, and the alphabetic shift key. When an interval extraction technique is used, the recipient must also know the interval used for extraction.

Listing 4.11. Deciphering the message created using CIPHER6.BAS through the use of the DCIPHER6.BAS program.

```
PROGRAM CIPHER6.BAS DECIPHERS A MESSAGE USING ONE
OF THE FOLLOWING TECHNIQUES TO FORM A CIPHER ALPHABET
```

```
(1) INTERVAL EXTRACTION SEQUENCE
(2) SIMPLE TRANSPOSITION SEQUENCE
(3) NUMERIC TRANSPOSITION SEQUENCE


Enter method to form enciphered message 1, 2, or 3: 1
Enter the interval as a numeric between 1 and 25: 3
Enter keyword or keyword phrase in UPPERCASE: MAYDECEMBER


Plaintext-based alphabet is : ABCDEFGHIJKLMNOPQRSTUVWXYZ
Keyword-based alphabet is : MAYDECBRFGHIJKLNOPQSTUVWXZ
Interval alphabet is : YCFILPTWMDBGJNQUXAERHKOSVZ
Enter UPPERCASE Alphabetic Shift Key: B
Shifted keyword mixed alphabet is : GJNQUXAERHKOSVZYCFILPTWMDB
Enter filename to store plaintext message, default=MESSAGE.DAT
Enter filename to store enciphered message, default=CIPHERTX.DAT
Select keyboard (k) or file (f) message input: F
Press Return key to display resulting deciphered message




Resulting deciphered message is:
TO FIDEL
FROM GORBY
PLEAS ENOTE THATA FEWCH ANGES
INTHE EASTN OWWAR RANTY OURCO
NSIDE RATIO NOFCH ANGIN GCUBA
NECON OMYTO THECA PITAL ISTIC
SYSTE MSTOP OTHER WISER EMEMB
ERFAM OUSFA TEOFR OMANI ANLEA
DERST OPBES TREGA RDSST OPXXX
```

Because I'm not a good typist, file input was selected in place of keyboard input when I wrote this book. Because the program was created using the same PRTOUT subroutine used by enciphering programs to display the resulting deciphered message, that message is displayed in groups of five characters.

The inclusion of PRINT statements to display the four alphabets developed by the program can be used to trace the operation of the program. In addition, you can use the positional relationship between the plaintext alphabet characters and the characters in the shifted keyword mixed alphabet to verify the deciphering of the message contained in Listing 4.10 into the plaintext shown at the bottom of Listing 4.11. For example, the first group of five enciphered characters in Listing 4.10 are YOUGI. Locating Y in the shifted keyword mixed alphabet in Listing 4.11 and reading upward to the plaintext alphabet results in the extraction of the character P. Similarly, O becomes L, U becomes E, G becomes A, and I becomes S. Thus, if you desire, you can easily verify the operation of the program. Once you are satisfied with its operation or do not wish to probe its operation, you can remove the extraneous print statements that display the different alphabets.

MONOALPHABETIC COMBINATIONS

Regardless of the technique or techniques used to form a monoalphabetic cipher alphabet, the maximum number of trials necessary to correctly decipher a message remains the same—26, which is approximately 4.0329E+26 (a very large number). However, that large number can be very deceptive, as it is relatively easy for a trained cryptanalyst to decipher a lengthy message with frequency analysis of the characters in the enciphered message. For example, E is the most common letter in the English language, followed by the letter T, which has the next highest frequency of occurrence. By performing a frequency analysis of the characters in an enciphered message, a trained analyst may be able to note that E was replaced by one character, T by another, and so on. By deciphering a few characters correctly, patterns may become visually identifiable. Deciphering three enciphered characters as EET, for example, may provide the analyst with a clue that the character prefixing the first deciphered E is the plaintext M. This monoalphabetic

substitution weakness means that you should keep messages relatively short to hinder frequency analysis. This weakness, however, led to the development of polyalphabetic substitution encipherment and pseudorandom encipherment techniques—topics I'll cover in the next two chapters of this book.

One of the more interesting matrix-based enciphering techniques operates on pairs of characters to reduce the potential for a frequency analysis. Although referred to as the Playfair cipher after Lyon Playfair, a Victorian scientist and the deputy speaker of the House of Commons, in actuality, the cipher was developed by Playfair's friend and close associate Charles Wheatstone.

The Playfair cipher system is based upon the formation of a keyword mixed alphabet that is contained in a 5 x 5 matrix, where the letters I and J are regarded as identical and combined to reduce the English alphabet to 25 letters. Thus, the use of the keyword QUALE produces the following alphabetic matrix used for encipherment:

Q	*U*	*A*	*L*	*E*
B	*C*	*D*	*F*	*G*
H	*I/J*	*K*	*M*	*N*
O	*P*	*R*	*S*	*T*
V	*W*	*X*	*Y*	*Z*

The encipherment of messages occurs using pairs of letters— a technique referred to as digraphic *encipherment. The rules governing the encipherment of each pair of characters is based on the relationship of the letters to one another in the keyword-based matrix. Because there are only three possible relationships between letters in the matrix, there are three rules that govern encipherment.*

If a pair of letters falls within the same row, they are replaced by the letters to their right, with each row considered cyclical so that the letter to the right of the last letter in a row becomes

continues

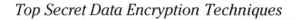

continued

the first letter in the row. Thus, the pair of letters ST is replaced by TO, and QU is replaced by UA.

The second rule governing the encipherment of pairs of letters is applicable to letters that appear in the same column. Similar to the rule governing the replacement of pairs of letters contained in the same row, letters that appear in the same column are replaced by the letter beneath each letter. Here, the cyclical provision results in the letter below the last letter in the column being the letter at the top of the column. Thus, DR is enciphered as KX, and ZE is enciphered as EG.

The third rule governing encipherment is applicable to the situation in which a pair of plaintext letters is not located in a common row or column. When this occurs, each letter is replaced by the letter located in its own row at the column position occupied by the other plaintext letter. Thus, under this rule, DE is replaced by GA, and TH is replaced by ON.

To further reduce the ability of frequency analysis as a decipherment tool, any double letter occurring in a pair is separated by an X. Thus, HOLLY becomes HOLXLY if the pair of L letters is on a pair boundary.

The use of digraphs by the Playfair cipher extends the cipher combinations from 26 letters when a one-for-one monoalphabetic substitution process is used to either 625 or 676 digraphs, depending upon the manner in which the I/J letter combination is used. Not only does this technique provide a substantial expanded base of characters for a frequency analysis, it also forces an analysis to be performed on letter pairs whose frequency of occurrence has substantially less divergence than single letters. For example, the two most common letters in the English language, E and T, have an average frequency of approximately 12 percent and 9 percent, respectively. In comparison, the two most common letter pairs, TH and HE, have a frequency of occurrence of 3.5 percent and 2.5 percent.

During World War II, the Playfair cipher was used by Australian coast watchers hiding on many Japanese-occupied islands in the South Pacific. Using the keys ROYAL NEW ZEALAND NAVY and PHYSICAL EXAMINATION, messages were transmitted concerning the loss of PT 109, which lead to the rescue of Lieutenant John F. Kennedy and his crew.

5

POLYALPHABETIC SUBSTITUTION

The conclusion of Chapter 4, "Transposition-Based Mono-alphabetic Substitution," briefly discussed a major weakness of monoalphabetic substitution-based enciphering techniques. That weakness is its susceptibility to frequency analysis— a relatively long message can be used as a guide for a trial-and-error process in which the most commonly occurring letters in a plaintext alphabet are substituted for the most frequently occurring characters in the enciphered message. A trained cryptanalyst can use this technique as a wedge to further deciphering operations because the correct substitution of one plaintext character for an enciphered character is carried through the entire enciphered message when a monoalphabetic substitution process is employed.

One method used to overcome the weakness of a mono-alphabetic substitution system is the use of a polyalphabetic substitution system. Unlike a monoalphabetic substitution system in which each plaintext character is mapped into a fixed ciphertext character, a polyalphabetic substitution system permits each plaintext character to be mapped to a different ciphertext character for a specified number of occurrences (before being mapped back into its original ciphertext character). The number of different ciphertext

characters each plaintext character can be mapped to depends on the number of ciphertext alphabets used. This number defines the period or cyclic redundancy of repetition of the mapping process.

Although a manual enciphering process becomes more difficult to perform as the number of ciphertext alphabets increases, the use of computers significantly reduces this difficulty. This chapter examines the construction and utilization of several polyalphabetic substitution systems. Similar to previous chapters, this chapter shows you how to construct enciphering and deciphering programs to automate the use of polyalphabetic substitution systems to encipher and decipher messages. This chapter also discusses several variations you may wish to consider when developing different types of polyalphabetic substitution systems.

Lawyer and architect Leon Battista Alberti is considered by many to be the father of Western cryptology. The author of the most comprehensive manuscript on cryptanalysis for its time, Alberti is also credited with the invention of polyalphabetic substitution and enciphered code in the fifteenth century.

Alberti's efforts in the development of a polyalphabetic substitution system took the form of a disk constructed with two copper plates. The circumference of each plate was divided into 24 equal parts known as cells. The larger copper plate, which was stationary, contained the letters of the alphabet entered into each cell in alphabetic sequence. The letters H, K, and Y were not included (Alberti did not feel they were necessary). Because the letters J, U, and W were not in his alphabet, he inscribed the numbers 1 to 4 to complete the entries in the cells of the fixed plate.

The second plate, which had a smaller diameter than the stationary plate, had 24 cells into which the letters of the Latin alphabet were inscribed in a random order. This plate

was movable and was placed over the larger plate (the plates attached to one another by a needle affixed through the center of each plate). The needle provided a relationship between the movable and fixed-plate cell entries.

Alberti's cipher disk enabled the relationship between the plaintext alphabet contained on the circumference of the fixed plate and the ciphertext alphabet contained on the circumference of the movable plate to be altered. To do so simply required the placement of a letter in the movable disk so it was positioned toward a letter on the outer disk. Because each new setting of Alberti's disk created a new cipher alphabet, each setting altered the plaintext-ciphertext encipherment relationship and enabled encipherment to occur using a polyalphabetic substitution process. All that was required to successfully encipher and decipher messages was for each party to have identical disks and to agree on the initial index letter of the movable disk and a method to change the use of the index.

SIMPLE POLYALPHABETIC SUBSTITUTION SYSTEMS

One of the earliest polyalphabetic substitution systems is known as the Vigenére cipher, named after its inventor, Blaise de Vigenére. First published in 1586, the Vigenére cipher is based on the development of a tableau in which all possible displaced alphabets are positioned one under another with the original alphabet placed in the top row.

THE VIGENÉRE CIPHER

Listing 5.1 illustrates the basic Vigenére tableau, which consists of 26 rows (each row contains 26 letters). Note that the Vigenére tableau can be represented as a *26 x 26* matrix consisting of 676 elements. In fact, the tableau contained in Listing 5.1 was created by executing the POLY1.BAS program (see Listing 5.2).

Listing 5.1. The basic Vigenére tableau.

```
   ABCDEFGHIJLKMNOPQRSTUVWXYZ

A  ABCDEFGHIJLKMNOPQRSTUVWXYZ
B  BCDEFGHIJLKMNOPQRSTUVWXYZA
C  CDEFGHIJLKMNOPQRSTUVWXYZAB
D  DEFGHIJLKMNOPQRSTUVWXYZABC
E  EFGHIJLKMNOPQRSTUVWXYZABCD
F  FGHIJLKMNOPQRSTUVWXYZABCDE
G  GHIJLKMNOPQRSTUVWXYZABCDEF
H  HIJLKMNOPQRSTUVWXYZABCDEFG
I  IJLKMNOPQRSTUVWXYZABCDEFGH
J  JLKMNOPQRSTUVWXYZABCDEFGHI
K  KLMNOPQRSTUVWXYZABCDEFGHIJ
L  LMNOPQRSTUVWXYZABCDEFGHIJK
M  MNOPQRSTUVWXYZABCDEFGHIJKL
N  NOPQRSTUVWXYZABCDEFGHIJKLM
O  OPQRSTUVWXYZABCDEFGHIJKLMN
P  PQRSTUVWXYZABCDEFGHIJKLMNO
Q  QRSTUVWXYZABCDEFGHIJKLMNOP
R  RSTUVWXYZABCDEFGHIJKLMNOPQ
S  STUVWXYZABCDEFGHIJKLMNOPQR
T  TUVWXYZABCDEFGHIJKLMNOPQRS
U  UVWXYZABCDEFGHIJKLMNOPQRST
V  VWXYZABCDEFGHIJKLMNOPQRSTU
W  WXYZABCDEFGHIJKLMNOPQRSTUV
X  XYZABCDEFGHIJKLMNOPQRSTUVW
Y  YZABCDEFGHIJKLMNOPQRSTUVWX
Z  ZABCDEFGHIJKLMNOPQRSTUVWXY
```

Listing 5.2. The POLY1.BAS program listing.

```
REM PROGRAM POLY1.BAS
DIM PLAINTEXT$(26), TABLEAU$(26, 26)
        CLS
GOSUB INITIALIZE
GOSUB TABLE
GOSUB PRINTIT
END
```

```
INITIALIZE:
        RESTORE
        REM Initialize plaintext values
        FOR I = 0 TO 25
        READ PLAINTEXT$(I)
        NEXT I
        DATA "A","B","C","D","E","F","G","H","I","J","K","L","M","N"
        DATA "O","P","Q","R","S","T","U","V","W","X","Y","Z"
RETURN
TABLE:
        FOR J = 0 TO 25
        FOR I = 0 TO 25
        TABLEAU$(J, I) = PLAINTEXT$((I + J) MOD 26)
        NEXT I
        NEXT J
RETURN
PRINTIT:
        PRINT "   ";
        FOR I = 0 TO 25: PRINT PLAINTEXT$(I); : NEXT I: PRINT :
PRINT
        FOR J = 0 TO 25
        PRINT PLAINTEXT$(J); " ";
        FOR I = 0 TO 25
        PRINT TABLEAU$(J, I);
        NEXT I
        PRINT
        NEXT J
RETURN
```

THE POLY1.BAS PROGRAM

The POLY1.BAS program uses the INITIALIZE subroutine to
initialize the letters of the alphabet into the string array
PLAINTEXT$. The subroutine TABLE is used to fill the two-dimen-
sional string array labeled TABLEAU$ with a sequence of 26 alpha-
bets. Through the use of a nested pair of FOR-NEXT loops and a MOD
26 operator, each row in the string array TABLEAU$ is assigned an
alphabet in which Row *n* has a displacement of one character

position with respect to Row *n*-1. To illustrate the operation of the subroutine TABLE, note that when J is 0, I varies from 0 to 25. Thus, the use of TABLEAU$(J,I) gives Row 0 the assigned values of PLAINTEXT$((I+0)MOD26), the non-displaced alphabet. Once the inner I loop is completed, J is incremented by 1 to a value of 1 and the I loop is again varied from 0 to 25. This results in TABLEAU$(J,I) having Row 1 assigned the alphabet displaced by one position because PLAINTEXT$((I+J)MOD26) results in a value of 1 for J shifting the assignment of plaintext letters to TABLEAU$ by one position.

The subroutine PRINTIT was created to print the tableau as well as the row and column labels that represent vertically and horizontally positioned alphabets. This subroutine was developed simply to display the tableau, and its row and column positioning elements were used for the extraction of characters from the tableau during the enciphering process.

ENCIPHERMENT

To use the Vigenére cipher system, first select a keyword or keyword phrase. This keyword or keyword phrase, unlike those used in a keyword-based, mixed alphabet, can retain repeating characters. For example, SECRET is a valid Vigenére cipher keyword, although it would be modified to SECRT if used to develop a keyword-based, mixed alphabet.

Once the Vigenére keyword or keyword phrase is selected, it is repeated in tandem with the characters in the plaintext message as the plaintext message is encoded. On a repeating basis, one character from the plaintext message and one character from the keyword are used as row and column header indices. The location within the tableau where the indices intersect points to the ciphertext character that is extracted from the tableau.

Listing 5.3 illustrates an example of a Vigenére encipherment using the keyword SECRET. Due to the symmetrical structure of the tableau, you can use either the row or column for the

plaintext character pointer and the opposite row or column for the keyword character pointer. For example, using the plaintext character for the row position and the keyword character for the column position extracts the ciphertext character E when the plaintext character is M and the keyword character is S. If you reverse the assignment of rows and columns, the use of the column character M and the row character of S as pointers also extracts of the ciphertext character E.

Although the use of a Vigenére cipher negates the use of a letter frequency count as a decipherment wedge by a crypt-analyst, this cipher system has one serious deficiency. This deficiency is known as the "probable word" attack in which a cryptanalyst first selects a word considered likely to be in the plaintext message. Then the cryptanalyst performs a modulo 26 subtraction of each character in that word from all possible locations in the ciphertext, examining the sequence of characters produced by the modulo 26 subtraction process for a recognizable word or word fragment.

Listing 5.3. A Vigenére encipherment.

```
Keyword:      SECRETSECRETSECRETSECRE

Plaintext:    MEETMEINSTLOUISTOMORROW
Ciphertext:   EIGKQXARUKPHMMUKSFGVTFA
```

During World War I, the Italians used an encipher system known as cifrario tascabile, *or "pocket cipher," that was a modified Vigenére cipher with the digits added to the end of the plaintext alphabet (the cipher alphabets consisted of the digits 10 to 45 in sequence). Radiograms intercepted by the Austrians that were enciphered using the* cifrario tascabile *usually required less than half a day for trained cryptanalysts to decipher, and they provided them with a wealth of information, including the ability to respond to an Italian offensive before the offensive was launched!*

OTHER POLYALPHABETIC SUBSTITUTION METHODS

As previously explained, a major weakness of the Vigenére cipher system is its susceptibility to a probable word attack. This susceptibility results from the use of a repeating keyword whose characters are continuously used as pointers with each plaintext character for the extraction of a ciphertext character from the tableau. To counter this susceptibility, you can develop a large number of different polyalphabetic substitution methods. An examination of the major elements of a periodic polyalphabetic substitution system, however, may be more useful at this point.

PERIODIC POLYALPHABETIC SUBSTITUTION

A periodic polyalphabetic substitution system contains one plaintext alphabet and two or more cipher alphabets. The plaintext alphabet is considered the primary alphabet because it serves as an extraction pointer to a column location within each cipher alphabet row. The cipher alphabets provide the characters for extraction that yield the ciphertext, and they are referred to as secondary alphabets.

Listing 5.4 illustrates a simple example of a periodic polyalphabetic substitution system. In this example, the plaintext alphabet is the sequential English alphabet (A through Z) with position one commencing with the letter A. The secondary cipher alphabets are a sequence of five plaintext alphabets shifted by one, two, three, four, and five character positions. The first cipher alphabet is indicated by the row header C1, and succeeding cipher alphabets are indicated by the row headers C2, C3, C4, and C5.

Listing 5.4. The periodic polyalphabetic substitution system.

```
Plaintext alphabet:
    ABCDEFGHIJKLMNOPQRSTUVWXYZ
```

```
Cipher alphabets:

C1    BCDEFGHIJKLMNOPQRSTUVWXYZA

C2    CDEFGHIJKLMNOPQRSTUVWXYZAB

C3    DEFGHIJKLMNOPQRSTUVWXYZABC

C4    EFGHIJKLMNOPQRSTUVWXYZABCD

C5    FGHIJKLMNOPQRSTUVWXYZABCDE
```

OPERATION

The operation of a periodic polyalphabetic substitution system involves locating the plaintext character in the plaintext alphabet. Locate the match position that serves as a pointer to the extraction of a cipher character from the first cipher alphabet. The second plaintext character is then matched against the plaintext alphabet, and the match position serves as a mechanism to extract the second cipher character from the second cipher alphabet. This process continues until a character is extracted from the last cipher alphabet. At this point the process begins anew and the next plaintext match causes an extraction to occur from the first cipher alphabet.

To illustrate the use of a periodic polyalphabetic substitution system, encipher the message FIRE FRED using the system illustrated in Listing 5.4. Locating F in plaintext and using that character location as a pointer to the first cipher alphabet (C1) extracts the cipher character G. Locating I in the plaintext and using its position as a pointer to the second cipher alphabet (C2) extracts the cipher character K. Similarly, R is enciphered as U, E is enciphered as H, and F is enciphered as J. Because you have now used the last cipher alphabet, encipher R, which is the sixth character in the plaintext message, using the first cipher alphabet—R is enciphered as S. Similarly, E is enciphered using the second cipher alphabet as G, and D is enciphered using the third cipher alphabet to obtain its replacement character G. Thus, the message FIRE FRED is enciphered as GKUIKSGG.

In the example shown in Listing 5.4, there was a total of five cipher alphabets. This means that the use of each cipher alphabet is repeated for every five characters in the plaintext—this polyalphabetic substitution system is then said to have a period

of five. Unfortunately, this also means that if a cryptanalyst can determine the repetition period of the cipher alphabets, he or she can perform a series of character frequency analyses that could eventually decipher an intercepted message. To add a degree of difficulty to the life of a cryptanalyst, you can use a variety of techniques to reduce the potential threat of analysis and decipherment.

REDUCING THE PROBABILITY OF DECIPHERMENT

One method that can be used to reduce the potential threat of analysis and decipherment is to extend its repetition period. Although this is time consuming when performed manually and subject to an increased probability of an enciphering error as the number of cipher alphabets increases, you can easily accomplish this through automation with a computer. Because you should also eliminate the use of a simple displacement for creating the cipher alphabets, you can use several methods to accomplish this. First, you can base the creation of the plaintext and each ciphertext alphabet on the use of a keyword or keyword phrase. For example, if you use the keyword MICROSOFT for the plaintext alphabet and the keyword phrase WINDOWS ARE FUN for the ciphertext alphabets, you can use the first keyword in its normal manner, and the second keyword can be used vertically as a mechanism to establish shifted cipher alphabets.

Listing 5.5 illustrates the use of a keyword-based, periodic polyalphabetic substitution system using the keyword MICROSOFT to form the plaintext alphabet; the keyword phrase WINDOWS ARE FUN is used to form shifted cipher alphabets. You should note that the plaintext keyword-based alphabet on the top portion of Listing 5.5 serves as a position pointer to each cipher alphabet. Concerning the cipher alphabet, you should note that because I will shortly develop a program using 26 cipher alphabets incorporated into a matrix, I labeled the cipher alphabets 0 to 25 to correspond to the array index that will be used. You should also note that the use of a vertical keyword or keyword phrase to form cipher alphabets positions the keyword or keyword phrase characters to the extreme right of the matrix in the last column.

For example, in cipher alphabet 0, W is rotated to the last column; thus, the first column commences with the character X. Similarly, in Row 1 (cipher alphabet 1) the character I in the keyword phrase WINDOWSAREFUN is positioned in the last column, which makes the character J the first character in Row 1.

Listing 5.5. A plaintext keyword-based alphabet and polyalphabetic ciphertext matrix using a shifted keyword-based alphabet.

```
   MICROSFTABDEGHJKLNPQUVWXYZ

0  XYZABCDEFGHIJKLMNOPQRSTUVW
1  JKLMNOPQRSTUVWXYZABCDEFGHI
2  OPQRSTUVWXYZABCDEFGHIJKLMN
3  EFGHIJKLMNOPQRSTUVWXYZABCD
4  PQRSTUVWXYZABCDEFGHIJKLMNO
5  TUVWXYZABCDEFGHIJKLMNOPQRS
6  BCDEFGHIJKLMNOPQRSTUVWXYZA
7  STUVWXYZABCDEFGHIJKLMNOPQR
8  FGHIJKLMNOPQRSTUVWXYZABCDE
9  GHIJKLMNOPQRSTUVWXYZABCDEF
10 VWXYZABCDEFGHIJKLMNOPQRSTU
11 CDEFGHIJKLMNOPQRSTUVWXYZAB
12 DEFGHIJKLMNOPQRSTUVWXYZABC
13 HIJKLMNOPQRSTUVWXYZABCDEFG
14 IJKLMNOPQRSTUVWXYZABCDEFGH
15 KLMNOPQRSTUVWXYZABCDEFGHIJ
16 LMNOPQRSTUVWXYZABCDEFGHIJK
17 MNOPQRSTUVWXYZABCDEFGHIJKL
18 NOPQRSTUVWXYZABCDEFGHIJKLM
19 QRSTUVWXYZABCDEFGHIJKLMNOP
20 RSTUVWXYZABCDEFGHIJKLMNOPQ
21 UVWXYZABCDEFGHIJKLMNOPQRST
22 WXYZABCDEFGHIJKLMNOPQRSTUV
23 YZABCDEFGHIJKLMNOPQRSTUVWX
24 ZABCDEFGHIJKLMNOPQRSTUVWXY
25 ABCDEFGHIJKLMNOPQRSTUVWXYZ
```

One weakness of polyalphabetic substitution systems was discovered by Auguste Kerckhoffs, a Dutchman born in 1835 who became a naturalized citizen of France. Author of La Cryptographie militaire, *considered one of the most extensive works on cryptanalysis, Kerckhoffs developed a general solution for polyalphabetic substitution systems that has deciphered many "unbreakable" messages.*

Under the Kerckhoffs method, a group of several intercepted messages is aligned so that the position of each enciphered character in each message is aligned by column. If the same key is used for the encipherment of each message, the letters in each column represent an encipherment process in which the same ciphertext alphabet was used. Thus, each column can be attacked as if it represented a monoalphabetic substitution by performing a frequency analysis of the letters in each column. Of course, if you change the key used to govern the enciphering process, the frequency of key changes and the number of messages enciphered by any one key determines the ability of the Kerckhoffs process to be used against your messages. If you transmit only a few messages with each key prior to changing the key, a frequency analysis of your messages on a column-by-column basis will more than likely produce meaningless results. If you transmit a large number of messages but change keys frequently, your message groups enciphered by a common key will probably be sufficient for a cryptanalyst to apply Kerckhoffs' method. Thus, you must balance both the change in keys and the number of messages enciphered using a key.

THE POLY2.BAS PROGRAM

Now that you have reviewed a few techniques to construct a series of cipher alphabets, I'll show you how to develop a program to encipher a message using a polyalphabetic substitution technique. This program is located on the file POLY2.BAS on the convenience disk, and for simplicity of illustration, it uses 26 cipher alphabets.

Listing 5.6 contains the main portion of POLY2.BAS. After using four PRINT statements to display information about the program, the first INPUT statement assigns the plaintext keyword or keyword phrase to the string variable TEXT$. The subroutine INITIALIZE is then invoked to form the plaintext alphabet, and the subroutine KEYWORD is invoked to form a keyword-based, mixed alphabet. This is followed by a FOR-NEXT loop that assigns the keyword-based, mixed alphabet to the string array PLAIN$ (the string array PLAINTEXT$ will be reused). Once the ciphertext keyword or keyword phrase is entered, it is assigned to the string variable TEXT$ and the subroutines INITIALIZE and KEYWORD are invoked again to form the ciphertext keyword-based, mixed alphabet. This alphabet is placed into the array CIPHER$ with a FOR-NEXT loop. A series of four subroutines is then invoked. Subroutines PFORMCIPHER and PCONVERTSTORE are modified versions of the subroutines FORMCIPHER and CONVERTSTORE (the prefix P is used to denote its modification for polyalphabetic use). The MSGFILE and PRTOUT subroutines remain the same.

Listing 5.6. The main portion of the POLY2.BAS program.

```
REM PROGRAM POLY2.BAS
DIM PLAINTEXT$(26), PLAIN$(26), CIPHER$(26), CIPHERTEXT$(26),
KEY$(26)
        CLS
        PRINT "POLY2.BAS PROGRAM enciphers text based upon the
        ↪use of two keywords"
        PRINT "or keyword phrases using a polyalphabetic substi-
        ↪tution process using"
        PRINT "26 cipher alphabets."
        PRINT
        INPUT "Enter plaintext keyword or keyword phrase in
UPPERCASE: ", TEXT$
GOSUB INITIALIZE                        'initialize plaintext
                                        ↪alphabet

GOSUB KEYWORD                           'form keyword based mixed
                                        ↪alphabet
```

continues

Listing 5.6. Continued

```
        FOR I = 0 TO 25: PLAIN$(I) = PLAINTEXT$(I): NEXT I
        INPUT "Enter ciphertext keyword or keyword phrase in
UPPERCASE: ", TEXT$
GOSUB INITIALIZE                         're-initialize plaintext
                                           ➥alphabet
GOSUB KEYWORD
        FOR I = 0 TO 25: CIPHER$(I) = PLAINTEXT$(I): NEXT I
GOSUB PFORMCIPHER                        'create 26 cipher alpha-
                                           ➥bets
GOSUB MSGFILE                            'assign I/O files, place
                                           ➥message on a file
GOSUB PCONVERTSTORE                      'convert and store
                                           ➥ciphertext on a file
GOSUB PRTOUT                             'print results
END
```

THE SUBROUTINE PFORMCIPHER

Listing 5.7 illustrates the statements contained in the subroutine PFORMCIPHER. As noted in the REM statement at the beginning of this subroutine, its function is to form 26 ciphertext alphabets using the first keyword character as a basis to generate each alphabet.

Listing 5.7. The subroutine PFORMCIPHER.

```
PFORMCIPHER:
        REM routine to form 26 CIPHERTEXT alphabets based on the
first keyword character
        FOR ZI = 0 TO 25
        GOSUB INITIALIZE
        FOR J = 0 TO 25
        IF CIPHER$(ZI) = PLAINTEXT$(J) THEN GOTO GOTYA
        NEXT J
GOTYA:  J = J + 1
        FOR K = 0 TO 25
        CIPHERTEXT$(ZI) = CIPHERTEXT$(ZI) + PLAINTEXT$((K + J)
MOD 26)
```

```
        NEXT K
        NEXT ZI
    RETURN
```

The subroutine PFORMCIPHER contains three FOR-NEXT loops. The outer loop uses the index ZI, which varies from 0 to 25 and is used to develop 26 ciphertext alphabets. After the first FOR statement, invoke the subroutine INITIALIZE to set the plaintext alphabet in its sequence into the array PLAINTEXT$. The FOR-NEXT loop using the index J then compares the character in the appropriate location of the string array CIPHER$ to each character in PLAINTEXT$ until a match occurs. When a match occurs, the character in the string array CIPHER$, which represents the first character in the ciphertext alphabet ZI, is matched to position J in the plaintext alphabet and a branch to the label GOTYA occurs. Because you want to shift the matched character to the last column, increment J by 1 prior to using the FOR-NEXT loop with K as the index to form the ciphertext alphabet. The execution of the subroutine PFORMCIPHER produces the 26 × 26 character matrix illustrated in Listing 5.5 (CIPHERTEXT$(ZI) varies from 0 to 25 when WINDOWSAREFUN is used as the ciphertext keyword phrase).

THE SUBROUTINE PCONVERTSTORE

The subroutine PCONVERTSTORE is similar to the subroutine CONVERTSTORE, although it is modified to sequentially pick a ciphertext character from each cipher alphabet in sequence until the last alphabet is reached. The ciphertext character extraction process begins anew with the first cipher alphabet.

Listing 5.8 contains the statements in the subroutine PCONVERTSTORE. The statement that sets the variable C to a value of 0 also sets the pointer to the first cipher alphabet. The next modification to CONVERTSTORE is the replacement of the string array PLAINTEXT$ with the string array PLAIN$ in the first IF statement in the subroutine. This statement mates a character from the plaintext stored in the string variable TEXT$ to a character in the string variable PLAIN$, which contains the keyword-based, mixed, plaintext alphabet. When a match occurs, J points

to the location in the keyword-based, mixed alphabet that serves as a pointer to each cipher alphabet for the extraction to a cipher character. However, when you branch to the label GOTIT, you must increment J by 1 because you incremented J by that amount in the subroutine PFORMCIPHER.

Listing 5.8. The subroutine PCONVERTSTORE.

```
PCONVERTSTORE:
        REM Routine to convert and store ciphertext on a file
        OPEN INFILE$ FOR INPUT AS #1
        OPEN OUTFILE$ FOR OUTPUT AS #2
        C = 0                             'first alphabet pointer
        DO UNTIL EOF(1)
                INPUT #1, TEXT$
                MSGLEN = LEN(TEXT$)
                IF MID$(TEXT$, 1, 1) = "/" THEN GOTO CLEARTXT
                IF MID$(TEXT$, 1, 1) = "\" THEN GOTO DONE1
                REM Convert plaintext to ciphertext
                    FOR I = 1 TO MSGLEN
                    FOR J = 0 TO 25
                    IF MID$(TEXT$, I, 1) = PLAIN$(J) THEN
GOTO GOTIT
                    NEXT J
GOTIT:              MID$(TEXT$, I, 1) = MID$(CIPHERTEXT$(C),
J + 1, 1)
                    C = C + 1
                    IF C = 26 THEN C = 0      'reset to first
                                                     alphabet
                    NEXT I
CLEARTXT:           WRITE #2, TEXT$
        LOOP
DONE1:      CLOSE #2
RETURN
```

Once a match occurs and you branch to the label GOTIT, the character in the string TEXT$ is replaced by a character from the cipher alphabet whose index value is C at position J+1 through the use of the MID$ statement. C is then incremented by 1 to

point to the next cipher alphabet. However, if C equals 26 it is reset to a value of 0 to point back to the first cipher alphabet.

PROGRAM EXECUTION

Listing 5.9 illustrates an example of the execution of POLY2.BAS using MICROSOFT as the plaintext keyword and WINDOWSAREGREAT as the ciphertext keyword phrase. I purposely changed the ciphertext keyword from WINDOWSAREFUN to WINDOWSAREGREAT to illustrate one deficiency of keyword-based polyalphabetic substitution systems: common keywords or keyword phrases. (The POLY2.BAS program enciphers text based on the use of two keywords or keyword phrases using a polyalphabetic substitution process using 26 cipher alphabets.)

Listing 5.9. The execution of POLY2.BAS.

```
Enter plaintext keyword or keyword phrase in UPPERCASE:
MICROSOFT
Enter ciphertext keyword or keyword phrase in UPPERCASE:
WINDOWSAREGREAT
Enter filename to store plaintext message, default=MESSAGE.DAT
Enter filename to store enciphered message, default=CIPHERTX.DAT
Select keyboard (k) or file (f) message input: K
Enter your message - place a / at the beginning of each line
that should remain in plaintext and a \ on a separate line
to indicate the end of the enciphered message

/TO ROSS THE BOSS
/FROM JODY
YOU CONFUSED PICK UP THE BALL AND GET
OFF THE COURT WITH THE QUOTE WHEN THE
GOING GETS TOUGH THE TOUGH GET GOING
\
Press Return key to display resulting enciphered message


Resulting enciphered message is:
```

continues

Listing 5.9. Continued

```
TO ROSS THE BOSS
FROM JODY
VNIGT KHMKR FUEJX EDTAB ACMOH
RHVZL TZHZS RXGXK PGMTA XEFPS
DHIFB PGAOD RKWTP TTRQT RKDHD
LKHBD ARBEI EJHMO
```

At this point it may be useful to manually encipher a portion of the cleartext YOU CONFUSED message to develop the enciphered message VNIGT KHMKR FUEJX . . . shown in the lower portion of Listing 5.9. Entering the keyword-based, mixed, plaintext alphabet at the top of Listing 5.5, locate Y and extract the character in the Y column from the first cipher alphabet to obtain the character V. Next, locate the character O in the keyword-based, mixed, plaintext alphabet and extract the character in the plaintext O column from the second cipher alphabet to obtain the character N. Similarly, U in the plaintext message extracts I from the third cipher alphabet and so on.

In Listing 5.5, the ciphertext keyword phrase WINDOWSAREFUN was used, and the ciphertext keyword phrase WINDOWSAREGREAT was used when the program POLY2.BAS was executed. Because both keyword phrases have the first 10 characters in common, of which 9 are used to form cipher alphabets due to a duplicate W, the first 9 cipher alphabets are the same for both keyword phrases. This means that the use of a polyalphabetic substitution system is more secure if you avoid industry-specific keywords or keyword phrases as well as other terms someone may be able to correctly guess based on your or other employee's work habits.

THE DPOLY2.BAS PROGRAM

Earlier in this chapter you developed the POLY2.BAS program to encipher messages using a polyalphabetic substitution technique. Because you need a mechanism to automate the decipherment of such messages, I'll now focus your attention on the

development of a program to reverse the encipherment process. I'll label this program DPOLY2.BAS to denote that it deciphers messages enciphered using the POLY2.BAS program.

Listing 5.10 contains the statements in the main portion of the DPOLY2.BAS program. When you examine Listing 5.10 you should note that the only difference between the main portion of program DPOLY2.BAS and POLY2.BAS are changes to the PRINT statements (essentially, "cipher" is replaced by "decipher," and the prefix of the two subroutines is replaced by the character D to denote major changes to previously developed subroutines without that prefix). Because the only subroutines that were significantly changed were MSGFILE and PCONVERTSTORE, I'll focus on these two subroutines.

Listing 5.10. The main portion of program DPOLY2.BAS.

```
REM PROGRAM DPOLY2.BAS
DIM PLAINTEXT$(26), PLAIN$(26), CIPHER$(26), CIPHERTEXT$(26),
KEY$(26)
        CLS
        PRINT "DPOLY2.BAS PROGRAM deciphers text previously
        ➥enciphered using two keywords"
        PRINT "or keyword phrases and a polyalphabetic substitu-
        ➥tion process using"
        PRINT "26 cipher alphabets."
        PRINT
        INPUT "Enter plaintext keyword or keyword phrase in
UPPERCASE: ", TEXT$
GOSUB INITIALIZE                         'initialize plaintext
                                         ➥alphabet
GOSUB KEYWORD                            'form keyword-based mixed
                                         ➥alphabet
        FOR I = 0 TO 25: PLAIN$(I) = PLAINTEXT$(I): NEXT I
        INPUT "Enter ciphertext keyword or keyword phrase in
UPPERCASE:", TEXT$
GOSUB INITIALIZE                         're-initialize plaintext
                                         ➥alphabet
GOSUB KEYWORD
```

continues

Listing 5.10. Continued

```
          FOR I = 0 TO 25: CIPHER$(I) = PLAINTEXT$(I): NEXT I
     GOSUB PFORMCIPHER                      'create 26 cipher alpha-
                                            ➥bets
     GOSUB DMSGFILE                         'assign I/O files, place
                                            ➥message on a file
     GOSUB DPCONVERTSTORE                   'convert and store
                                            ➥ciphertext on a file
     GOSUB PRTOUT                           'print results
     END
```

THE SUBROUTINE DMSGFILE

The major differences between the subroutine MSGFILE and the subroutine DMSGFILE are related to the assignment of the string variables OUTFILE$ and INFILE$. In DMSGFILE, these assignments are reversed from their assignment in MSGFILE. Because the contents of the subroutine DMSGFILE were described as part of the description of DCIPHER6.BAS and other programs in Chapter 4, you should refer to that chapter for information concerning this subroutine and the program listing.

THE SUBROUTINE DPCONVERTSTORE

The statements used to form the subroutine DPCONVERTSTORE are contained in Listing 5.11. Unlike the subroutine PCONVERTSTORE, which converts a plaintext message to ciphertext and stores the message in ciphertext on a disk file, DPCONVERTSTORE performs a reverse process. That is, the subroutine DPCONVERTSTORE converts an enciphered message to plaintext and stores the plaintext message on a disk file.

Listing 5.11. The subroutine DPCONVERTSTORE statement listing.

```
DPCONVERTSTORE:
     REM Routine to convert and store ciphertext on a file
     OPEN INFILE$ FOR INPUT AS #1
     OPEN OUTFILE$ FOR OUTPUT AS #2
     C = 0                          'first alphabet pointer
     DO UNTIL EOF(1)
```

```
                    INPUT #1, TEXT$
                    MSGLEN = LEN(TEXT$)
                    IF MID$(TEXT$, 1, 1) = "/" THEN GOTO CLEARTXT
                    IF MID$(TEXT$, 1, 1) = "\" THEN GOTO DONE1
                    REM Convert plaintext to ciphertext
                            FOR I = 1 TO MSGLEN
                            FOR J = 0 TO 25
                            IF MID$(TEXT$, I, 1) =
     MID$(CIPHERTEXT$(C), J + 1, 1) THEN GOTO GOTIT
                            NEXT J
     GOTIT:             MID$(TEXT$, I, 1) = PLAIN$(J)
                            C = C + 1
                            IF C = 26 THEN C = 0      'reset to first
                                                         alphabet
                            NEXT I
     CLEARTXT:          WRITE #2, TEXT$
              LOOP
     DONE1:      CLOSE #2
     RETURN
```

When you compare the subroutine DPCONVERTSTORE to the subroutine PCONVERTSTORE, you should note that the difference between the two subroutines is limited to the structure of an IF statement in each subroutine and the statement at label GOTIT. In PCONVERTSTORE, the first IF statement is used to match each character in the string variable TEXT$ to a character in the keyword-based, mixed alphabet stored in the array PLAIN$ and uses the location of the match as a pointer to a cipher alphabet. In the subroutine DPCONVERTSTORE each character is matched to the cipher alphabet whose value is C at position J+1.

In the subroutine PCONVERTSTORE, a branch to the label GOTIT results in the replacement of a plaintext character (MID$(TEXT$,I,1)) by a ciphertext character (MID$(CIPHERTEXT$(C),J+1,1)) in the cipher alphabet C at position J+1. In the subroutine DPCONVERTSTORE, you should replace each enciphered character with its equivalent plaintext character. Because a match using the previously described IF

statement results in the location of the correct alphabet and the location within the alphabet, set each character in TEXT$ to the array element PLAIN$(J) to extract the appropriate plaintext character. This allows you to convert the ciphertext back into its equivalent plaintext character.

PROGRAM EXECUTION

To verify the operation of the program DPOLY2.BAS, execute it using the same plaintext and ciphertext keywords used to encipher your message using the POLY2.BAS program. Listing 5.12 illustrates the execution of the DPOLY2.BAS program using the plaintext keyword MICROSOFT and the ciphertext keyword phrase WINDOWSAREGREAT. The lower portion of this example shows the resulting deciphered message. You should note that this message is the same message that was entered as plaintext when the program POLY2.BAS was executed in Listing 5.9.

Listing 5.12. The execution of the DPOLY2.BAS program.

```
DPOLY2.BAS PROGRAM deciphers text previously enciphered using
➡two keywords or keyword phrases and a polyalphabetic substitu-
➡tion process using 26 cipher alphabets.


Enter plaintext keyword or keyword phrase in UPPERCASE:
MICROSOFT
Enter ciphertext keyword or keyword phrase in UPPERCASE:
WINDOWSAREGREAT
Enter filename to store plaintext message, default=MESSAGE.DAT
Enter filename for enciphered message, default=CIPHERTX.DAT
Select keyboard (k) or file (f) message input: F
Press Return key to display resulting deciphered message


Resulting deciphered message is:
TO ROSS THE BOSS
FROM JODY
```

```
YOUCO NFUSE DPICK UPTHE BALLA
NDGET OFFTH ECOUR TWITH THEQU
OTEWH ENTHE GOING GETST OUGHT
HETOU GHGET GOING
```

Other differences between DPOLY2.BAS and POLY2.BAS relate to PRINT statements changed to display "deciphered" instead of "enciphered" in the subroutine PRTOUT. Because this is an insignificant change, I did not change the name of the subroutine; however, the PRINT statements in the subroutine were changed when the program was stored on the file DPOLY2.BAS on the convenience disk.

6

USING RANDOM NUMBERS

Through the use of random numbers you can decrease the decipherment capability of people who illicitly gain access to an enciphered message. In fact, the use of a true random number sequence as an enciphering key theoretically makes it impossible for a person to decipher a message. Unfortunately, the use of a true random number sequence is beyond the capability of most organizations due to time, cost, and the effort required to provide the sequence to others that must use it to decipher messages. Thus, most random number sequences are actually pseudorandom number sequences that, with varying degrees of difficulty, can be duplicated.

This chapter discusses the ways in which true random number sequences are developed and why they are impractical for most persons and organizations. This chapter also examines the built-in random number generator included in most programming languages and the ways you can use that facility to create a pseudorandom number sequence that can serve as an enciphering and deciphering key. This discussion is followed by the construction of a series of programs that illustrates the use of computer-generated random number sequences to encipher and decipher messages.

RANDOM NUMBERS AND RANDOM NUMBER SEQUENCES

Random numbers are unordered numbers that are independent of preceding and succeeding numbers. A random number sequence is an unordered series of random numbers.

The use of random number sequences in cryptology provides a mechanism to create an unbreakable enciphered message. To illustrate this, assume that the random number sequence you obtain (through a process described later in this chapter) is converted into a binary sequence and that each plaintext character in your message is converted into a binary sequence. You can use modulo 2 addition to add the plaintext and random number binary values to produce an enciphered binary sequence. If the recipient has the same random number sequence, he or she could use modulo 2 subtraction to subtract the binary values of the random numbers from the enciphered binary sequence to reproduce the plaintext message. Because the binary random number sequence functions as a unique key known only to the message encipherer and the message decipherer, any person who illicitly obtains a copy of the enciphered message cannot decipher the message.

The father of the application of modulo 2 arithmetic to encipherment systems was Gilbert Vernam. Working in downtown Manhattan for American Telephone & Telegraph Company during 1917, Vernam was assigned to a project to investigate the security of the telegraph.

In 1917 the Baudot code was used for the transmission of information by telegraph. In this code, characters are represented by a predefined sequence of a combination of five marks and spaces that represent different levels of current that are placed on the telegraph line to identify a character. Automated telegraph operations used punched paper tape for

both offline message preparation as well as message transmission and reception. Marks were represented by holes, and spaces were represented by leaving the tape intact.

After studying telegraph operations, Vernam proposed punching a "key" tape consisting of randomly selected characters literally pulled from a hat. He proposed electromechanically adding the pulses on the keytape to the pulses of plaintext characters as follows:

plaintext		*key*	*ciphertext*
mark	+	mark	= space
mark	+	space	= mark
space	+	mark	= mark
space	+	space	= space

With Vernam's method, if you assign a binary 1 to a mark and a binary 0 to a space, you have modulo 2 addition forming the ciphertext. Thus, it should not be surprising that Vernam's method for reconstructing the plaintext characters was based on modulo 2 subtraction.

Vernam's encipherment ideas were converted from paper to hardware by the construction of two devices during 1918. These devices were connected to two teletypewriters, and their successful use marked the beginning of automated cryptographic operations.

GENERATING RANDOM NUMBER SEQUENCES

A true random number sequence is not only an unordered sequence of numbers but also a nonreproducible sequence. According to rumors, certain spy agencies monitor natural processes, such as the height of solar flares on the sun or the number of gamma rays emitted by decaying radioactive material per unit period of time, to develop a sequence of

nonreproducible random numbers. These numbers are converted to a binary sequence for use as a key by equipment manufactured to encipher and decipher messages. Disks or tapes containing random binary sequences that serve as an enciphering and deciphering key are then prepared for use during different time periods, and those disks are sent by courier to government locations where communications security (COMSEC) equipment that uses such disks are located. COMSEC personnel then load the appropriate disks at predefined times to change the keys (the duplicate use of a binary key sequence eliminates the reproducibility of the key and enchiphers the messages using a repeating key susceptible to decipherment by foreign governments monitoring communications).

The time, effort, and cost associated with developing true random number sequences and distributing those sequences for use normally restricts its use to government institutions. Commercial products that encipher messages and data files normally use pseudorandom number sequences.

PSEUDORANDOM NUMBER SEQUENCES

A pseudorandom number sequence is based on the use of an algorithm to generate a sequence of numbers. Any person that has access to the algorithm can exercise the algorithm and eventually reproduce the pseudorandom number sequence used by another person. Although this means that the use of pseudorandom number sequences makes an enciphered message decipherable by an unauthorized party, the time and effort required to do so may preclude this from actually happening. Some algorithms, for example, may generate millions to hundreds of billions of unique key sequences, forcing persons who illicitly obtain access to an enciphered message to use powerful mainframe computers for months or years in an attempt to decipher a message. The selection of an algorithm to generate pseudorandom numbers can provide a very high level of security even though the resulting enciphered message based on the use of that algorithm is breakable. One algorithm that provides

a reasonable number of random number sequences is built into the BASIC programming language in the form of the RND function.

THE *RND* FUNCTION

The BASIC RND function invokes a routine that generates pseudo-random decimal numbers in the range 0 to 1. In most versions of BASIC, including QuickBASIC, the format of the RND function is RND[(x)], where the value of x determines how the function generates the next random number. Table 6.1 indicates the number returned by the function based on different argument values.

Table 6.1.
The returned *RND* function number.

Argument Value	Number Returned
x<0	Always returns the same number for any given x
x>0 or x omitted	Returns the next random number in the sequence
x=0	Returns the last number generated

When using the RND function in a program with a value of x>0, the same sequence of random numbers is generated each time you execute the program. This generation is illustrated in Listing 6.1 (the top portion lists a simple program that prints five random numbers using the RND function; the lower portion shows the results obtained from executing the program three times). Note that each sequence of random numbers generated by the program is exactly the same.

Listing 6.1. Using the **RND** *function.*

```
FOR I = 1 TO 5
PRINT RND(I);
NEXT I
PRINT
```

continues

Listing 6.1. Continued

.7055475	.533424	.5795186	.2895625	.301948
.7055475	.533424	.5795186	.2895625	.301948
.7055475	.533424	.5795186	.2895625	.301948

Using random numbers to encipher and decipher messages dates to modern espionage. During World War II, Nazi agents, as well as Allied spies working in occupied Europe and in neutral countries, enciphered and deciphered messages based on the use of what is known as a one-time pad.

Each one-time pad consists of a series of pages with each page containing a sequence of random numbers, usually blocked into groups of five digits for convenience. Each page of random numbers is used one time.

To use this method, a spy first prepares his or her message in plaintext, positioning the characters in the message into groups of five letters. Then the value of each letter in the group is added (using modulo 26 arithmetic) to the value of each random digit to produce the enciphered message. The following example illustrates the enciphering operation attributed to agent Maxwell Smart:

plaintext message	SENDM	OREMO	NEYNO	WXXXX
random digits	15829	31276	50341	92371
modulo 26 addition				
enciphered message	TJVFV	RSGTU	SEBRP	FZAEY

The received message is decoded through the use of a second one-time pad whose contents match the contents of the pad used by the spy. For example, the received enciphered message would be deciphered as follows:

received message	TJVFV	RSGTU	SEBRP	FZAEY
random digits	15829	31276	50341	92371
modulo 26 subtraction	SENDM	OREMO	NEYNO	WXXXX

> *Unless the one-time pad falls into the hands of enemy agents, the resulting enciphered message is unbreakable. This technique is so secure that its use was documented in many spy trials during the Cold War, although the capture of spies was attributed to factors other than the ability of counteragents to read enciphered messages.*

THE *RANDOMIZE* STATEMENT

The use of an easily duplicable random number sequence clearly limits its usefulness as an encryption and decryption key. Fortunately, BASIC contains a statement that can be used to reseed the random number generator and produce a different sequence of random numbers. The statement that reseeds the random number generator is the RANDOMIZE statement whose format is RANDOMIZE[expression].

If the optional expression in the RANDOMIZE statement is omitted, BASIC pauses and displays the message "Random Number Seed (–32768 to 32767)?" To change the sequence of random numbers generated by the use of a RND function, you can place a RANDOMIZE statement at the beginning of a program. Listing 6.2 illustrates this concept (the top portion of the listing contains a small program listing that includes the RANDOMIZE statement; the lower portion of the listing shows the results of executing the program three times). Note that the use of a different seed results in the generation of a new random number sequence.

Listing 6.2. Using the **RANDOMIZE** *statement.*

```
RANDOMIZE
FOR I = 1 TO 5
PRINT RND(I);
NEXT I
PRINT

Random-number seed (-32768 to 32767)? -5
.4362451   .3257061   .2495473   .1388514   .1759562
```

continues

Listing 6.2. Continued

```
Random-number seed (-32768 to 32767)? -5
.4362451   .3257061   .24965473   .1388514   .1759562
Random-number seed (-32768 to 32767?) 0
.7641413   .3576428   .1068624   .7075312   4.804176E-02
```

Because the value of the random number seed can range from −32,768 to 32,767, you can obtain the capability to generate 65,536 different random number sequences using the RANDOMIZE statement. You can consider using a variable with a RANDOMIZE statement. Reading the value for the variable from the keyboard serves as a mechanism to provide a program user with the capability to specify the random number sequence to encipher and decipher messages. The seed value then becomes the "code" or "key" for the enciphering and deciphering process.

WORKING WITH RANDOM NUMBERS

Because a majority of the applications for random numbers are for numbers in some range other than 0 to 1, you need a mechanism to change those numbers to integers. That mechanism is obtained by multiplying the value of RND by $10n$, where n defines the number of integers you need from 1 to 6. Then you can use the BASIC INT function to obtain the integer value of the resulting computation. For example, INT(RND*100) produces integers whose values are between 0 and 99, and INT(RND*1000) produces integers whose values are between 0 and 999.

THE RANDOM1.BAS PROGRAM

The top portion of Listing 6.3 contains the program listing of RANDOM1.BAS. The lower portion shows the results obtained when the program is executed three times. This program generates random numbers between 0 and 25 based on the use of the RND function and reseeds the random number generator by specifying a reseeding position. You should note that the program simply discards any number exceeding 25 to smooth the resulting random numbers to the range 0 to 25.

*Listing 6.3. The RANDOM1.BAS program listing and sample execution with different values assigned to the **RANDOMIZE** statement.*

```
REM Program RANDOM1.BAS
REM routine to generate random numbers between 0 and 25
CLS
start: INPUT "Enter a number (enter 0 to terminate): ", y
       IF y = 0 THEN STOP
       RANDOMIZE (y)
       FOR I = 1 TO 75
       x = INT(RND(I) * 100)
       IF x > 25 THEN GOTO skip
       PRINT x;
skip:  NEXT I
       PRINT
       GOTO start


Enter a number, 0 to terminate: 5
23 7 19 18 22 6 17 15 1 3 17 23 20 13 14
Enter a number, 0 to terminate: 7
11 5 16 20 16 3 15 4 4 23 4 4 24 23 21 19 8 3 11 6 3
Enter a number, 0 to terminate: 9
1 14 14 22 7 22 7 19 23 4 20 9 2 23 5 15 11
Enter a number, 0 to terminate: 0
```

THE RANDOM2.BAS PROGRAM

Listing 6.4 contains the program listing and sample execution of the RANDOM2.BAS program. This simple program was developed to illustrate how you can use random numbers to encipher messages. In this example, the plaintext alphabet is restricted to the 26 uppercase letters. This alphabet is initialized by the INITIALIZE subroutine. The program uses a user-entered number to seed the random number generator and accepts a one-line message read into the string variable TEXT$. The characters in that message are then placed into the string array KEY$.

Listing 6.4. The RANDOM2.BAS program listing and its repeated execution using different random seed numbers and the same plaintext message.

```
REM Program RANDOM2.BAS
REM Sample program to demonstrate use of random numbers for
➡enciphering
DIM KEY$(80), PLAINTEXT$(26)
CLS
        PRINT "Program RANDOM2.BAS to demonstrate use of random
          ➡numbers and"
        PRINT "random number seed in enciphering operations"
GOSUB INITIALIZE
START: PRINT
        INPUT "Enter a random seed number (enter 0 to terminate): ", Y
        IF Y = 0 THEN STOP
        RANDOMIZE (Y)
        INPUT "Enter a one-line message in UPPERCASE: ", TEXT$
        FOR I = 1 TO LEN(TEXT$)
        KEY$(I) = MID$(TEXT$, I, 1)
        NEXT I
REM Encipher
        PRINT "Enciphered message is                 : ";
        FOR I = 1 TO LEN(TEXT$)
        FOR J = 0 TO 25
        IF PLAINTEXT$(J) = KEY$(I) GOTO GOTIT        'locate charac-
                                                       ➡ter position
        NEXT J                          'in plaintext array
GOTIT: X = INT(RND * 100)               'get random number
        IF X > 25 THEN GOTO GOTIT       'less than 25
        Z = (J + X) MOD 26              'use MOD 26 addition to add
        PRINT PLAINTEXT$(Z);            'display enciphered character
        NEXT I
        GOTO START
INITIALIZE:
        RESTORE
        REM Initialize plaintext values
```

```
          FOR I = 0 TO 25
          READ PLAINTEXT$(I)
          NEXT I
          DATA "A","B","C","D","E","F","G","H","I","J","K","L","M","N"
          DATA "O","P","Q","R","S","T","U","V","W","X","Y","Z"
RETURN
```

```
Program RANDOM2.BAS to demonstrate use of random numbers and
random number seed in enciphering operations

Enter a random seed number, 0 to terminate 5
Enter a one-line message in UPPERCASE: FIREFREDNOW
Enciphered message is : CPKWBXVSORN
Enter a random seed number, 0 to terminate 8
Enter a one-line message in UPPERCASE: FIREFREDNOW
Enciphered message is : RDMXNQVCJXE
Enter a random seed number, 0 to terminate 51
Enter a one-line message in UPPERCASE: FIREFREDNOW
Enciphered message is : ZXDDMCBNHGZ
Enter a random seed number, 0 to terminate 0
```

The routine labeled ENCIPHER matches each character in the message that was placed in the string array KEY$ to a plaintext character. When a match is found, a branch to the label GOTIT occurs, and a two-digit random number is obtained. The program then discards the random number if it exceeds 25 and obtains a new random number, forcing x to between 0 and 25.

Once an acceptable value of x is obtained, the index value of J, which represents the plaintext character location in the alphabet, is added with modulo 26 addition to the random number. By restricting the largest random number to 25 and the plaintext character position to 26, the largest number produced by adding the two becomes 51. Performing modulo 26 addition prevents a resulting number occurring from different additions

(the case if a random number added to the index resulted in a value of 52 or more). 1MOD26 is 1, for example, and so is 53MOD26 and 79MOD26. By limiting the maximum value of the sum of the index and random number to 51, you ensure that you can correctly decipher a message using the technique previously described.

MODULO 26 ARITHMETIC

To better understand the routine necessary to decipher the previously enciphered series of messages that used a random number-based enciphering program requires a review of modulo 26 addition and modulo 26 subtraction. Suppose the position values of the first four characters in a plaintext message with respect to their location in the sequential plaintext alphabet are 6, 2, 4, and 18, and a randomly generated number sequence based on a defined seed was 12, 14, 22, and 17.

The top portion of Listing 6.5 illustrates the enciphering process performed through the use of modulo 26 addition. Once the enciphered characters reach their destination, the same sequence of random numbers is used to reconstruct the original characters. However, this time modulo 26 subtraction is performed as illustrated in the bottom portion of Listing 6.5. When performing modulo 26 subtraction, if the numerator is smaller than the subtrahend, you "borrow" 1, which in effect has a decimal value of 26, prior to performing the required subtraction. Thus, *9–17* becomes *(26+9)–17*, or *18*, when modulo 26 subtraction is performed.

Listing 6.5. Enciphering and deciphering using modulo 26 addition and subtraction.

Enciphering using modulo 26 addition

character value	6	2	4	18
random number	12	14	22	17
modulo 26 addition result				
represents enciphered character value	18	16	0	9

Deciphering using modulo 26 subtraction

enciphered character value	18	16	0	9
random number	12	14	22	17

modulo 26 subtraction result				
represents plaintext character value	6	2	4	18

Now that you have an appreciation of the modulo subtraction process, you should focus your attention on a small program developed to decipher a previously enciphered one-line message based on a specified seed for the BASIC random number generator.

THE DRANDOM2.BAS PROGRAM

Listing 6.6 contains the statements in the program DRANDOM2.BAS and three examples of its execution. In keeping with the filenaming conventions previously established, I labeled the program DRANDOM2.BAS to indicate that it deciphers a message previously enciphered using RANDOM2.BAS. (DRANDOM2.BAS closely resembles the program contained in Listing 6.4.)

Listing 6.6. The DRANDOM2.BAS program listing and its repeated execution using different random seed numbers and different ciphertext messages to re-create a common plaintext message.

```
REM Program DRANDOM2.BAS
DIM KEY$(80), PLAINTEXT$(26)
CLS
      PRINT "Program DRANDOM2.BAS to demonstrate use of random
      ➡numbers and"
      PRINT "random number seed in deciphering operations"
GOSUB INITIALIZE
START: PRINT
      INPUT "Enter a random seed number (enter 0 to terminate): ", Y
      IF Y = 0 THEN STOP
```

continues

Listing 6.6. Continued

```
          RANDOMIZE (Y)
          INPUT "Enter a one-line message in UPPERCASE: ", TEXT$
          FOR I = 1 TO LEN(TEXT$)
          KEY$(I) = MID$(TEXT$, I, 1)
          NEXT I
REM Decipher
          PRINT "Deciphered message is               : ";
          FOR I = 1 TO LEN(TEXT$)
          FOR J = 0 TO 25
          IF PLAINTEXT$(J) = KEY$(I) GOTO GOTIT
          NEXT J
GOTIT: X = INT(RND * 100)
          IF X > 25 THEN GOTO GOTIT
          IF J < X THEN J = J + 26
          Z = J - X
          PRINT PLAINTEXT$(Z);
          NEXT I
          GOTO START
INITIALIZE:
          RESTORE
          REM Initialize plaintext values
          FOR I = 0 TO 25
          READ PLAINTEXT$(I)
          NEXT I
          DATA  "A","B","C","D","E","F","G","H","I","J","K","L","M","N"
          DATA "O","P","Q","R","S","T","U","V","W","X","Y","Z"
RETURN


Program DRANDOM2.BAS to demonstrate use of random numbers and
random number seed in deciphering operations

Enter a random seed number, 0 to terminate 5
Enter a one-line message in UPPERCASE: CPKWBXVSORN
Deciphered message is: FIREFREDNOW
Enter a random seed number, 0 to terminate 8
```

```
Enter a one-line message in UPPERCASE: RDMXNQVCJXE
Deciphered message is: FIREFREDNOW
Enter a random seed number, 0 to terminate 51
Enter a one-line message in UPPERCASE: ZXDDMCBNHGZ
Deciphered message is: FIREFREDNOW
Enter a random seed number, 0 to terminate 0
```

After entering the random number generator's seed number and the one-line enciphered message, the decipher routine matches each character in the message against the plaintext alphabet stored in the array PLAINTEXT$. Once a match occurs, you have located the correct position value or location of the ciphertext character in the plaintext alphabet—a value assigned to the variable J. After the value of J is obtained, a branch to the label GOTIT occurs and a random number between 0 and 25 is extracted. Because you must perform modulo 26 subtraction to reconstruct the plaintext character, compare the value of J to the value of *x* and increase J by 26 if the value of J is less than *x*. Then subtract the value of *x* from the value of J, in effect performing modulo 26 subtraction. As indicated in the lower portion of Listing 6.6, this process enables you to reconstruct the plaintext message.

A comparison of the execution of RANDOM2.BAS and DRANDOM2.BAS contained in the lower portions of Listings 6.4 and 6.6 verifies the validity of the deciphering process. That is, plaintext messages enciphered using a defined random number seed value in Listing 6.4 are entered as ciphertext messages in Listing 6.6 with the same seed number. This correctly deciphers each message into its original plaintext contents.

CONSTRUCTING AN ENCIPHERING PROGRAM

Now that you have reviewed the operation and utilization of the BASIC RANDOMIZE statement and the RND function, you have the foundation that enables you to construct an enciphering program that uses the built-in BASIC random number generator.

However, because that random number generator is available to anyone that has a computer and the appropriate software, an intercepted enciphered message could be easily deciphered if you simply use a numeric value for selecting an available random number seed (there are a limited number of random number seeds from which you can select in comparison to the number of combinations obtained by mixing up an alphabet). Prior to creating your random number-based enciphering program, first focus your attention on extending the random process to obtain a much larger series of possible enciphering combinations.

EXTENDING THE RANDOM PROCESS

As previously mentioned in this chapter, the BASIC random number seed varies from –32,768 to 32,767 (providing a total of 65,536 random number sequences because a seed value of 0 also produces a sequence). Therefore, a person who intercepts or otherwise obtains a copy of your enciphered message can decipher that message by trying each random number seed. This obviously takes time; however, it subjects the contents of your enciphered message to decipherment through the use of a well-known maximum number of decipherment attempts.

There are numerous methods you can consider to extend the level of security when using BASIC's random number generator. For example, to obtain an additional level of security you can consider using two key numbers in your encipherment and decipherment process. The first key number, as previously explained, selects the random number seed. The second number either directly or indirectly sets the beginning location in the random number sequence selected. This process could theoretically result in an infinite number of combinations an unauthorized person might be faced with during an illegal decipherment process.

The top portion of Listing 6.7 contains a routine designed to generate random numbers between 0 and 25 based on a defined seed and location within the selected seed. The bottom portion of Listing 6.7 shows the results obtained by executing the program three times. Each time the program was executed, the

same seed was used but the position in the seed was changed using a FOR-NEXT loop in which the statement dummy=RND is executed *x* times, where *x* represents the value of the location in the seed. The first random number considered for use by the program is located at position *x*+1 in the selected seed.

Listing 6.7. The routine to generate a random number sequence based on a defined seed and a location in the seed.

```
REM routine to generate random numbers between 0 and 25
REM based on a defined seed and location in the seed

start: INPUT "Enter your key numbers separated by commas: ", y, x
       RANDOMIZE (y)
       FOR  i = 1 to x: dummy = RND: NEXT i
       FOR i = 1 to 75
       x = INT(RND(i) * 100)
       IF x > 25 THEN GOTO skip
       PRINT x;
skip:  NEXT i
       PRINT


Enter your key numbers separated by commas: 1,1
 10  10  10  5  21  22  11  4  5  18  21  15  17  8  15  13  15  9
Enter your key numbers separated by commas: 1,50
 17  8  15  13  15  9  10  16  12  18  6  0  15  9  23  5  11
Enter your key numbers separated by commas: 1,100
 15  9  23  5  11  3  14  2  10  13  6  4  10  10  23  22  5  11  13
➥8   2   21
```

The use of a FOR-NEXT statement to select a location in a random number sequence places a limit on the location within the sequence that you can begin your encipherment process (each version of BASIC has a limit on the maximum value that can be assigned to a variable). For example, the maximum value of an integer is 32,767 in QuickBASIC, and a long integer can have a value up to 2,147,483,647 in that language. You can also use single- or double-precision numeric variables to extend the maximum value allowed by the language and the number of

combinations allowed to select a position within a random number sequence. However, the use of high numbers, whether they are integers or numerics, can cause excessive user waiting time while the computer cycles through a large number of random numbers within a particular random number seed to locate the desired position within a random number sequence. For example, the execution of the FOR-NEXT loop FOR i = 1 TO x, shown at the top of Listing 6.7, could make the user of the program wait for several minutes if an extremely large value is entered for *x* and the program is executed on an old 8088-based computer.

In addition to a long waiting period, the use of a large number is difficult to remember and might restrict the use of the preceding example to a simple low value or easy-to-remember numbers such as 500, 1,000, and so on. The use of a number limited to 1,000 or so still significantly extends the number of combinations resulting from the selection of a random number sequence and position within the sequence. For 1,000 positions within a sequence, the total number of combinations an unauthorized person would need to try to decipher a message would be extended to 65,536,000 because there are 65,536 different random number seeds. Even if the right combination was discovered halfway through the search sequence, more than 32 million combinations would have to be used for the attempted decipherment. For a message such as BID THIRTY-TWO MILLION ON TUESDAY AT THE AUCTION, any decipherment that occurs after "TUESDAY" may be worthless. The use of two keys that select a random number sequence and position within the sequence may provide a significant level of message protection for most users. However, recognizing the need of most users for an extra level of protection, I'll demonstrate two easy-to-implement techniques that can be used to obtain that desired level of protection.

EXTENDING THE COMBINATIONS

You can substantially increase both the number of combinations available for starting the random number sequence to be

used in a program and the speed in which the user of the program obtains access to the sequence. To accomplish this, use a third key to be used by the program to increment the FOR-NEXT loop to both speed up the positioning process and increase the number of combinations an unauthorized party must try to decipher an enciphered message.

The top portion of Listing 6.8 contains the program listing for entering a three-number sequence to select a position within a random number sequence defined by a random number seed from which to commence the encipherment process at the next random number position. In this example, the first number is assigned to the variable x, and it is used to select the random number seed sequence. The second number entered is assigned to the variable y and defines the limit of the FOR-NEXT loop. The value of the third number entered is assigned to the variable z and defines the increment used in the FOR-NEXT loop. Each of the numbers can be considered to represent a key. You can consider this elementary program as a random number generator based on the use of a three-key sequence.

Listing 6.8. A sample program that uses three numbers to rapidly position the starting point within a random number sequence of a defined random number seed.

```
INPUT "Enter your three key numbers, each separated by a comma:
➥", x, y, z
RANDOMIZE x
For i = 1 TO y STEP z
dummy = RND
NEXT i
FOR i = 1 TO 10
PRINT INT(RND * 100);
NEXT i
PRINT

Enter your three key numbers, each separated by a comma: 12,24,4
 1  87  10  94  95  82  26  71  21  57
Enter your three key numbers, each separated by a comma: 12,24,9
```

continues

Listing 6.8. Continued

```
 50  27  89  1  87  10  94  95  82  26
Enter your three key numbers, each separated by a comma:
➥12,240,9
 31  88  52  70  32  72  70  37  95  12
Enter your three key numbers, each separated by a comma:
➥12,110543,43
 3  3  17  51  70  18  51  35  79  27
Enter your three key numbers, each separated by a comma:
➥110543,1993,12
 65  34  48  63  89  66  63  2  41  29
```

The lower portion of Listing 6.8 illustrates the results obtained from executing the program listed at the top of the illustration five times in sequence using different key combinations.

The first two examples illustrated at the bottom of Listing 6.8 could have used the month and day of the month for the first two keys and an hour for the third key. The third example could have used the Julian day for the day instead of the day of the month. In the fourth example, the second key could be a person's date of birth. In the fifth example, perhaps the first key could be a person's date of birth, and the second and third keys could be the current year and month.

Regardless of the manner in which values are assigned to each key, the use of three keys can provide an extremely large number of combinations. However, the key (no pun intended) to obtaining a large number of combinations is the mechanism used to generate key values. By selecting easy-to-remember but relatively large digit values for each of the three keys, you can force an unauthorized person with access to a deciphering program to obtain the power of a large mainframe computer to decipher your message. For example, using a date in the form of mmddyy for the first key, a year in the form of yyyy for the second key, and a number in the form of dd for the third key could result in up to 10 billion possible combinations an unauthorized person might have to try to decipher your message! Now that's

a significant order of magnitude beyond the 65,536 random number seed sequences, and it adds a degree of decipherment difficulty that corresponds to a level of protection afforded by many commercially available systems whose purchase price significantly exceeds the cost of this book.

PROGRAM DEVELOPMENT

The foundation used to develop enciphering and deciphering programs based on the use of Microsoft's QuickBASIC random number generator is a mechanism to obtain a position in the random number generator that is difficult to duplicate.

To develop a subroutine to obtain a difficult-to-duplicate position within the random number generator, you must consider (1) the number of character positions you will use in a code your program will operate upon to obtain a location in the random number generator and (2) the characters that can be used for each position. For example, a two-position code restricted to numerics is limited to containing values from 00 to 99, or 100 (10^2), combinations. If those two positions can contain alphanumeric characters, each position can contain 36 combinations, and the two positions represent a total of 36^2, or 1,296, combinations.

Table 6.2 lists the number of combinations resulting from the use of code lengths varying from 1 to 10 positions, with each position containing up to 10 (numeric only), 26 (alphabetic only), 36 (alphanumeric), and 128 (any ASCII) permissible characters. As indicated in Table 6.2, an expansion of the number of code positions and/or the number of characters permitted to be entered in each position significantly increases the possible number of code combinations. Because most people can easily remember a six-position code, use this type of code to develop a mechanism to obtain a difficult-to-duplicate position within the built-in BASIC random number generator. Using six positions and allowing alphanumeric characters to be placed in each position produces 2,176,782,336 possible combinations! If you extend the characters that can be placed into each code position to the normal ASCII code, you would obtain $439*10^{10}$

possible combinations. Because characters should be converted to their ASCII numeric representation to use for positioning purposes, you need a mechanism to perform this operation.

Listing 6.9 illustrates a short segment of code to read characters and display their ASCII values. In this example, the program executes continuously until a break occurs. After reading a string that is assigned to the string variable A$, the program obtains the length of the string. A FOR-NEXT loop then extracts each character from the string with the MID$ function and prints the ASCII value of each character with the ASC function. The lower portion of Listing 6.9 illustrates the resulting ASCII values of each character from six strings entered as codes. Note that the code can be all alphabetic (GODAWGS), numeric (362436), alphanumeric (NINE9), or that it can include special characters such as the exclamation mark that are included in the normal ASCII character set (POWER!).

Table 6.2.
Code combinations based on code length
and characters allowed.

X	10^X	26^X	36^X	128^X
1	100.00E-01	260.00E-01	360.00E-01	128.00E+00
2	100.00E+00	676.00E+00	129.60E+01	163.84E+02
3	100.00E+01	175.76E+02	466.56E+02	209.72E+04
4	100.00E+02	456.98E+03	167.96E+04	268.44E+06
5	100.00E+03	118.81E+05	604.66E+05	343.60E+08
6	100.00E+04	308.92E+06	217.68E+07	439.80E+10
7	100.00E+05	803.18E+07	783.64E+08	562.95E+12
8	100.00E+06	208.83E+09	282.11E+10	720.58E+14
9	100.00E+07	542.95E+10	101.56E+12	922.34E+16
10	100.00E+08	141.17E+12	365.62E+13	118.06E+19

Listing 6.9. Using ASCII character values.

```
CLS
START:
        INPUT A$
        X = LEN(A$)
```

```
        FOR I = 1 TO X
        PRINT ASC(MID$(A$, I, 1)); " ";
        NEXT I
        PRINT
GOTO START

? GODAWGS
 71   79   68   65   87   71   83
?YEATIGERS
 89   69   65   84   73   71   69   82   83
? 362436
 51   54   50   52   51   54
? POWER!
 80   78   87   69   82   33
? NINE9
 78   73   78   69   57
? $39.99
 36   51   57   46   57   57
?
```

At this point it may be useful to examine a six-position code used to perform a series of manipulations to obtain a position within a random number seed. Although I'll review one series of manipulations, a six-character code provides 6!, or 720, possible methods by which the characters can be used if they are used one character at a time. You can change the method of code-character manipulation to fit specific requirements.

To manipulate six-position code, first multiply the ASCII value of each of the first two characters in the code to use as the RANDOMIZE seed setting. Multiply the ASCII values of the third and fourth characters in the code to serve as a first limit for entry into a position within the selected seed. Use the ASCII value of the fifth code character to increment toward the limit. As a further offset into the random number sequence, multiply the ASCII values of the fifth and sixth code characters and use the result as a second limit. Then sequence toward that limit using the ASCII value of the fourth code character as a mechanism for incrementing toward that limit.

Top Secret Data Encryption Techniques

The use of the six-code character grouping previously discussed is illustrated graphically in Figure 6.1. An analysis of the combinations obtained from the use of that code is warranted, as it indicates how good intentions can go astray and why many persons throughout the history of mankind have become so involved in developing "unbreakable" techniques that they literally couldn't see the trees in the forest and did not understand the weakness they created in their quest for increasing the complexity of their code design.

Figure 6.1.
Using the code characters.

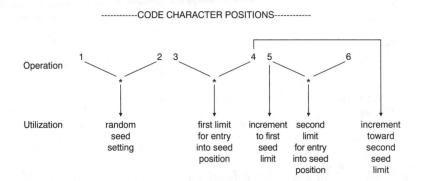

In Figure 6.1 the use of a two-character position to generate a seed setting when each position is restricted to alphanumeric characters reduces the number of seed combinations to 36^2, or 1,296, which is significantly less than the maximum number of seed settings supported in BASIC. The entry into the selected seed is based on the multiplication of the value of code positions 3 and 4, which are added to the product of the values of code positions 5 and 6. This means that the maximum value of the displacement into the selected seed is 2,592 positions when code positions are limited to alphanumeric characters. Thus, the maximum number of combinations one has to try in an attempt to locate the position within a selected seed for enciphering a message becomes 1,296 seeds * 2,592 positions, or 3,359,232 combinations! Although this is still a formidable number, it is certainly less formidable than the maximum number of combinations that can be obtained from a six-character position code. You may wish to consider alternative methods to

use the characters in a code to initiate a random number sequence within a seed at a defined position.

Later in this chapter I discuss an alternative method you can consider for the use of the characters in a code to initiate a sequence of random numbers. However, for the moment, I'll focus on the way you can code the previously described code-character manipulations for use in programs that encipher and decipher messages based on the use of the built-in BASIC random number generator. I'll also develop programs that accept any ASCII character in each code position (this significantly extends the number of possible combinations others must try to decipher a message enciphered with the RANDOM3.BAS program developed later in this chapter). For example, with each character code position capable of containing any conventional ASCII character, the use of code positions 1 and 2 for selecting the seed increases the number of seeds capable of being used to 127 * 127, or 16,129. Once you have an appreciation for the coding and operation of "secret" code-based programs, you'll learn how you can make those "secret" codes even less vulnerable.

THE POSITION.BAS PROGRAM

The top portion of Listing 6.10 contains the statements in the demonstration program POSITION.BAS, which accepts a "secret" code up to six characters in length and uses the ASCII values of those characters in the manner previously discussed as a mechanism for positioning into a place in the random number generator. In this program, the subroutine SETUP actually performs the previously described manipulation of the ASCII value of each code character. The lower portion of Listing 6.10 illustrates the execution of the program using five different "secret" codes—the program displays the numeric (ASCII) value of each code character and the first five random numbers following the execution of the positioning subroutine. Any ASCII character can be used for each code character; however, control characters that are nonprintable are obviously not printed when used as code characters.

Listing 6.10. The program listing of POSITION.BAS and examples of its repeated execution.

```
REM Program POSITION.BAS demonstrates the positioning to a place
➥in the
REM random number generator based on a secret code up to 6
➥characters
CLS
AGN:
        INPUT "Enter your secret code (6 characters maximum) :
        ➥"; CODE$
        IF LEN(CODE$) > 6 THEN GOTO AGN
GOSUB SETUP
        PRINT "Numeric value of code characters : ";
        FOR I = 1 TO 6
        PRINT CODE(I); " ";
        NEXT I
        PRINT : PRINT "1st five random numbers : ";
        FOR I = 1 TO 5: PRINT RND; : NEXT I: PRINT : PRINT
        END
SETUP:
        REM routine to position random number generator
        FOR I = 1 TO LEN(CODE$)
        CODE(I) = ASC(MID$(CODE$, I, 1))
        NEXT I
        SEED = CODE(1) * CODE2
        MAX = CODE(3) * CODE(4)
        RANDOMIZE SEED
        FOR I = 1 TO MAX STEP CODE(5)                    'position
        ➥into sequence
        DUMMY = RND
        NEXT I
        FOR I = 1 TO CODE(5) * CODE(6) STEP CODE(4) 'further
        ➥offset into sequence
        DUMMY = RND
        NEXT I
    RETURN
```

```
Enter your secret code (6 characters maximum) : ? HELPME
Numeric value of code characters :   72    69    76    80    77    69
1st five random numbers :   .8671363   .33787422   .4237103
➡ .6096486   .9087062


Enter your secret code (6 characters maximum) : ? 9NINES
Numeric value of code characters :   57    78    73    78    69    83
1st five random numbers :   .4755153   .8707944   .8031864
➡ .3487226   .6214768


Enter your secret code (6 characters maximum): ? 382438
Numeric value of code characters :   51    56    50    52    51    56
1st five random numbers :   .944414   .949271   .5596389   .7912182
➡ 9.593111E-02


Enter your secret code (6 characters maximum) : ? 3CARDS
Numeric value of code characters :   51    67    65    82    68    83
1st five random numbers:   .4237103   .6096486   .9087062   .8784156
➡ .0561406


Enter your secret code (6 characters maximum) : ? helpme
Numeric value of code characters :   104    101    108    112    109   101
1st five random numbers:   .5051253   .7871563 m .9859242   .1925381
➡.3514438
```

THE RTEST.BAS PROGRAM

One of the concerns you may have at this point is the possibility that each random seed results in a sequence of repeating random numbers. To determine if this is a potential problem, a program was developed to generate the first five random numbers in a seed as two-digit integers and cycle through the seed looking for a match.

Listing 6.11 contains the statements in this program that is labeled RTEST.BAS. Listing 6.12 illustrates the results of the execution of RTEST.BAS when 1 was entered as the seed number. After half an hour, I terminated the execution of the program by entering a Ctrl-break key sequence because more than

1.4 million numbers had been tested without encountering a duplicate sequence of five numbers. With more than 64,000 possible seeds and more than 1.4 million nonrepeating random number sequences per seed, it is obvious that it is very difficult to duplicate a position selected by a thoughtful code word manipulated in a thoughtful manner.

Listing 6.11. The program listing of RTEST.BAS, which tests for a repeated sequence within a random number seed.

```
REM Random sequence test program RTEST.BAS
        CLS
        PRINT "TEST FOR 5 REPEATED DIGITS AT BEGINNING OF SEQUENCE"
        POSITION = 3
        INPUT "Enter random generator seed number "; x
        RANDOMIZE x
        FOR I = 1 TO 5  'get first five random numbers as 2-digit
        ➥integers
        A(I) = INT(RND * 100)
        NEXT I
        k = 1
again:  FOR I = 1 TO 5   'get next group of five random numbers
➥as 2-digit integers
        b(I) = INT(RND * 100)
        NEXT I
        FOR I = 1 TO 5    'do they match?
        IF A(I) <> b(I) THEN GOTO skip
        NEXT I
        LOCATE POSITION, 1
        PRINT "match occurred at number =", k
        POSITION = POSITION + 1
        GOTO again
skip:   k = k + (6 - I)
        LOCATE 1, 60
        PRINT "search at #"; k
        GOTO again
```

Listing 6.12. Sample execution of program RTEST.BAS.

```
TEST FOR 5 REPEATED DIGITS AT BEGINNING OF SEQUENCE          search
➥at # 1425317
Enter random generator seed number ? 1
```

Now that you have a subroutine that can be used for positioning with the BASIC random number generation routine, you can develop the enciphering program.

THE RANDOM3.BAS PROGRAM

Listing 6.13 contains the statements in the main portion of the enciphering program stored on the file RANDOM3.BAS. This program was constructed to encipher messages using the built-in BASIC random number generator using the previously described subroutine SETUP to obtain a difficult-to-duplicate position within the random number generator.

Listing 6.13. Statements in the main portion of the program RANDOM3.BAS.

```
REM Program RANDOM3.BAS
      CLS
      DIM PLAINTEXT$(25)
      PRINT "RANDOM3.BAS - A program which enciphers messages"
      PRINT "using the built-in BASIC random number generator"
      PRINT
RTN:
      INPUT "Enter your secret code (6 characters maximum) : ";
CODE$
      IF LEN(CODE$) > 6 THEN GOTO RTN
GOSUB INITIALIZE           'initialize plaintext values
GOSUB SETUP                'obtain random seed and position in
                               ➥ seed
GOSUB MSGFILE        'assign I/O files, place message on a file
GOSUB RCONVERTSTORE 'convert and store ciphertext on a file
GOSUB PRTOUT               'print results
      END
```

When you examine the statements contained in Listing 6.13, note that the only new subroutine is RCONVERTSTORE (the prefix R is the name of the subroutine used to identify its modification for use in the random program operation).

THE SUBROUTINE RCONVERTSTORE

Listing 6.14 lists the statements in the subroutine RCONVERTSTORE. The differences between this subroutine and the previously described CONVERTSTORE subroutine are the statements bounded by the FOR-NEXT loop.

Listing 6.14. Statements in the subroutine RCONVERTSTORE.

```
RCONVERTSTORE:
        REM Routine to convert and store ciphertext on a file
        OPEN INFILE$ FOR INPUT AS #1
        OPEN OUTFILE$ FOR OUTPUT AS #2
        DO UNTIL EOF(1)
            INPUT #1, TEXT$
            MSGLEN = LEN(TEXT$)
            IF MID$(TEXT$, 1, 1) = "/" THEN GOTO CLEARTXT
            IF MID$(TEXT$, 1, 1) = "\" THEN GOTO DONE1
            REM Convert plaintext to ciphertext
                FOR I = 1 TO MSGLEN
                X = INT(RND * 100)          'get 2-digit integer
                X = INT(X / 3.85)           'smooth to 0 to 25
                FOR J = 0 TO 25
                IF MID$(TEXT$, I, 1) = PLAINTEXT$(J) THEN GOTO
                ➥GOTIT
                NEXT J
GOTIT:                  MID$(TEXT$, I, 1) = PLAINTEXT((X + J) MOD
                        ➥26)
                NEXT I
CLEARTXT:       WRITE #2, TEXT$
        LOOP
DONE1:          CLOSE #2
        RETURN
```

When converting the subroutine for operation with random numbers, the statement X=INT(RND*100) obtains a one- or two-digit number between 0 and 99. The next statement lowers the maximum resulting value of the modified random number by dividing the number by 3.85 and taking the integer of the result. This smooths the random number to a value between 0 and 25, which is equivalent to the index values in the array string PLAINTEXT$ in which the plaintext alphabet is stored.

The inner FOR-NEXT loop that increments J from 0 to 25 compares each character from a line of input from file #1 to a letter in the string array PLAINTEXT$. When a match occurs, J represents the position in PLAINTEXT$ where the match occurred. The branch to the label GOTIT results in the MOD 26 addition of the value of J to the smoothed value of the extracted random number. The MOD 26 addition of X and J is then used as an index to extract a new character from the string array PLAINTEXT$, which is used to replace the plaintext character in TEXT$. The subroutine RCONVERTSTORE uses the plaintext character set as a mechanism to generate ciphertext based on the previously described algorithm.

Listing 6.15 illustrates the execution of the program RANDOM3.BAS. In this example, the code 9LIVES was used to obtain a position in the BASIC random number generator. Because the program uses the previously developed PRTOUT subroutine, the resulting enciphered message is printed in groups of five characters as illustrated at the bottom of Listing 6.15.

Listing 6.15. The execution of RANDOM3.BAS.

```
RANDOM3.BAS - A program which enciphers messages
using the built-in BASIC random number generator

Enter your secret code (6 characters maximum) : ? 9LIVES
Enter filename to store plaintext message, default=MESSAGE.DAT
Enter filename to store enciphered message, default=CIPHERTX.DAT
Select keyboard (k) or file (f) message input: K
```

continues

Listing 6.15. Continued

```
Enter your message - place a / at the beginning of each line
that should remain in plaintext and a \ on a separate line
to indicate the end of the enciphered message

/TO:   ALL REGIONAL OFFICE MANAGERS
FROM: PRESIDENT LES MISERABLES
PIXHK FQCZV FIZDH PUMJQ NYKQT
RIQSC YDABH RDYDI GVHCS AIFIL
XJUZS GQQUL NACRI JYJAK DPDXS
DJODB QVKTV PRFWO BWFPU ONETO
YCWTY YMLVD FFWOQ BWVEI GGZJM
QLLBE QUYJT MZOTL UFKCU SQZXX
```

THE DRANDOM3.BAS PROGRAM

To use consistent naming conventions, I labeled the program
that deciphers messages enciphered using RANDOM3.BAS
as DRANDOM3.BAS. Listing 6.16 contains the statements
in the main part of that program that are very similar to
RANDOM3.BAS. In fact, the only change (in addition to changes
in the words in strings located in the PRINT statements) is the
substitution of the subroutines DMSGFILE for MSGFILE and
RDCONVERTSTORE for RCONVERTSTORE.

Listing 6.16. Statements in the main portion of program DRANDOM3.BAS.

```
REM Program DRANDOM3.BAS
        CLS
        DIM PLAINTEXT$(25)
        PRINT "DRANDOM3.BAS - A program which deciphers messages"
        PRINT "using the built-in BASIC random number generator"
        PRINT "that were enciphered using the RANDOM3.BAS program"
        PRINT
RTN:
        INPUT "Enter your secret code (6 characters maximum) :
        ➥CODE$
        IF LEN(CODE$) > 6 THEN GOTO RTN
```

```
GOSUB INITIALIZE            'initialize plaintext values
GOSUB SETUP                 'obtain random seed and position in seed
GOSUB DMSGFILE              'assign I/O files, place message on a
                             ➥file
GOSUB RDCONVERTSTORE        'convert and store plaintext on a file
GOSUB PRTOUT                'print results
END
```

The subroutine DMSGFILE essentially adjusts I/O file references to the opposite of the subroutine MSGFILE. The subroutine RDCONVERTSTORE is very similar to the subroutine RCONVERTSTORE, although it converts ciphertext to plaintext instead of plaintext to ciphertext.

THE SUBROUTINE RDCONVERTSTORE

Listing 6.17 contains the statements in the subroutine RDCONVERTSTORE. In this subroutine a random number is extracted and smoothed to a value between 0 and 25 in the same manner as the subroutine RCONVERTSTORE. Each character in the string variable TEXT$ is matched to a character in the string array PLAINTEXT$ (the position of the match assigned to the variable J).

Listing 6.17. Statements in subroutine RDCONVERTSTORE.

```
RDCONVERTSTORE:
        REM Routine to convert and store plaintext on a file
        OPEN INFILE$ FOR INPUT AS #1
        OPEN OUTFILE$ FOR OUTPUT AS #2
        DO UNTIL EOF(1)
                INPUT #1, TEXT$
                MSGLEN = LEN(TEXT$)
                IF MID$(TEXT$, 1, 1) = "/" THEN GOTO CLEARTXT
                IF MID$(TEXT$, 1, 1) = "\" THEN GOTO DONE1
                REM Convert ciphertext to plaintext
                        FOR I = 1 TO MSGLEN
                        X = INT(RND * 100)      'get 2-digit integer
                        X = INT(X / 3.85)       'smooth to 0 to 25
                        FOR J = 0 TO 25
```

```
                              IF MID$(TEXT$, I, 1) = PLAINTEXT$(J) THEN GOTO
                              ➥GOTIT
                              NEXT J
         GOTIT:               IF J < X THEN J = J + 26
                              MID$(TEXT$, I, 1) = PLAINTEXT$((J - X) MOD 26)
                              NEXT I
         CLEARTXT:            WRITE #2, TEXT$
              LOOP
         DONE1:       CLOSE #2
         RETURN
```

To perform modulo 26 subtraction, the value of J is compared to the value of X. If J is less than X, J is incremented by 26. The value of X is then subtracted from J using modulo 26 arithmetic, and the resulting value is used as an index into the string array PLAINTEXT$. The character at the index position represents the plaintext character, and it is used to replace the ciphertext character in the variable TEXT$.

Listing 6.18 illustrates the operation of the program DRANDOM3.BAS. In this example the user simply enters a "secret" code and selects the default filenames and file input as the mechanism for reading the previously created enciphered message. The resulting deciphered message in the lower portion of Listing 6.18 is displayed in groups of five characters because the subroutine PRTOUT was used in the program.

Listing 6.18. The execution of program DRANDOM3.BAS.

```
DRANDOM3.BAS - A program which deciphers messages
using the built-in BASIC random number generator
that were enciphered using the RANDOM3.BAS program


Enter your secret code (6 characters maximum) : ? 9LIVES
Enter filename to store plaintext message, default=MESSAGE.DAT
Enter filename for enciphered message, default=CIPHERTX.DAT
Select keyboard (k) or file (f) message input: F
Press the Return key to display resulting deciphered message
```

```
Resulting deciphered message is:
TO:   ALL REGIONAL OFFICE MANAGERS
FROM: PRESIDENT LES MISERABLES
TOPRE VENTA CHAPT ERELE VENAL
LEMPL OYEES MUSTW ORKAD OUBLE
SHIFT CHRIS TMASD AYWIT HOUTP
AYSTO PMANA GERSA RERES PONSI
BLEFO RIMPL EMENT INGTH ISPOL
ICYST OPHAV EANIC EDAYS TOPXX
```

Readers from Missouri may be curious as to the effect of entering a different "secret" code during the execution of the program DRANDOM3.BAS. To illustrate the effect, I used the code 9lives instead of 9LIVES. What may appear to be a small code change is significant to the mechanism developed for positioning to a place into the BASIC random number generator. Listing 6.19 illustrates the effect of using the program DRANDOM3.BAS with an invalid secret code. If you compare the decipherment illustrated in Listing 6.18 to the decipherment illustrated in Listing 6.19, you should note that the use of an incorrect code results in a meaningless deciphered message. It is as important to keep your secret code secure as it is not to lose your code.

Listing 6.19. Using DRANDOM3.BAS with an incorrect code.

```
DRANDOM3.BAS - A program which deciphers messages
using the built-in BASIC random number generator
that were enciphered using the RANDOM3.BAS program

Enter your secret code (6 characters maximum) : ? 9lives
Enter filename to store plaintext message, default=MESSAGE.DAT
Enter filename for enciphered message, default=CIPHERTX.DAT
Select keyboard (k) or file (f) message input: F
Press Return key to display resulting deciphered message

Resulting deciphered message is:
TO:   ALL REGIONAL OFFICE MANAGERS
```

continues

Listing 6.19. Continued

```
FROM: PRESIDENT LES MISERABLES
KZXUS OUBQR CFOHX CTDZK SPXCP
DYYER WEBKG LGHLU WODDM IHMQK
AQLKH FSCKQ MSTEZ YWEJB FHEWH
UTMTX OWIJC DAIBB HZHKA RBBFJ
ILNET XEKQC XDOZG DFVCX HIYRP
LGCMW VUNRU VSVMO CQQKG GKVXX
```

AN ALTERNATIVE RANDOM PROCESS

A second process you can consider to generate random numbers for use in enciphering operations is based on the work of Gilbert Vernam (see the shaded box near the beginning of this chapter). Using Vernam's method, which he employed to develop a long random key from two relatively short random keys as a foundation, you can perform a similar operation through the use of two random seed numbers.

To develop this alternative process, assume that you retain the use of a six-character "secret" code word. You can use the ASCII values of the code word as a mechanism to select two random number seeds. For each seed selected, you can position yourself into the random number sequence and extract 1,000 random numbers from the first sequence and 999 from the second sequence. You can then develop a routine I called ROTOR that operates on the two random number sequences similar to Mr. Vernam's dual paper tape reader.

When Gilbert Vernam developed the first automatic enciphering system, random characters were literally pulled from a hat. This system was time-consuming, and it limited the number of random characters on the tape to 1,000. Vernam realized that looping the tape repeated the random character sequence used for encipherment operations every 1,000 characters. To overcome this weakness, Vernam designed a special tape reader that read two tapes consisting of randomly selected characters. The contents of each tape

were added to one another using modulo addition. When a cycle of the shorter tape was completed, the longer tape was repositioned by one character position and the sequence of modulo addition by character position was repeated. The longer tape contained 1,000 randomly selected characters, and the shorter tape contained 999 randomly selected characters, which resulted in the use of two tapes extending the random character key sequence to 999,000 before the sequence repeated.

By extending the random cipher key from 1,000 to 999,000 characters, the security of Vernam's automated enciphering system was significantly enhanced. This extension permitted hundreds to thousands of messages to be enciphered before a new pair of tapes was necessary to prevent the key from repeating.

THE ROTOR.BAS PROGRAM

Listing 6.20 contains the statements in the program ROTOR.BAS, which is used to illustrate how you can create your own random number sequence generating routine that can be considerably different from that contained in BASIC but is based on the use of the BASIC random number generator.

Listing 6.20. The ROTOR.BAS program listing.

```
REM PROGRAM ROTOR.BAS
REM This program constructs a new random number sequence of
➡numbers that range
REM in value from 0 to 99 based on the extraction of random numbers
➡from two
REM seeds whose location are based on the composition of a six-
➡position code word.
REM This sequence repeats after 999,000 characters with the same
➡secret code.
CLS
DIM R1(1000), R2(999)
```

continues

Listing 6.20. Continued

```
RTN:
          INPUT "Enter your secret code (6 characters maximum) : ";
          ➥CODE$
          IF LEN(CODE$) > 6 THEN GOTO RTN
GOSUB SETUP
          P1 = 0
          P2 = 1
          FOR K = 1 TO 500
GOSUB ROTOR
          NEXT K
STOP
SETUP:
          REM routine to extract two random number sequences
          ➥based on
          REM the composition of the secret code
          FOR I = 1 TO LEN(CODE$)
          CODE(I) = ASC(MID$(CODE$, I, 1))
          NEXT I
          SEED1 = CODE(1) * CODE(3)
          X1 = CODE(5)
          DO UNTIL X1 <= 4
                   X1 = X1 / 2
          LOOP
          SEED1 = SEED * X1
          SEED2 = CODE(2) * CODE(4)
          X2 = CODE(6)
          DO UNTIL X2 <= 4
                   X2 = X2 / 2
          LOOP
          SEED2 = SEED2 * X2
          RANDOMIZE SEED1
          MAX = CODE(1) * CODE(3) * CODE(5)
          FOR I = 1 TO MAX STEP CODE(2)                      'position into
                                                             ➥sequence

           DUMMY = RND
          NEXT I
```

```
        FOR I = 1 TO CODE(1) * 500 STEP CODE(3)        'go further into
                                                       ⇒sequence
         DUMMY = RND
        NEXT I
        FOR I = 1 TO 1000                              'obtain first
                                                       ⇒sequence
         R1(I) = RND                                   'of random numbers
        NEXT I
        RANDOMIZE SEED2
        MAX = CODE(2) * CODE(4) * CODE(6)
        FOR I = 1 TO MAX STEP CODE(4)                  'position into
                                                       ⇒ next sequence
         DUMMY = RND
        NEXT I
        FOR I = 1 TO CODE(4) * 8307 STEP CODE(2)       'go further into
                                                       ⇒sequence
         DUMMY = RND
        NEXT I
        FOR I = 1 TO 999                               'get second
                                                       ⇒sequence
          R2(I) = RND
        NEXT I
RETURN
ROTOR:
        R = INT(((R1(P1) + R2(P2)) * 100) MOD 99)
        PRINT USING "## "; R;
        P1 = P1 + 1
        IF P1 = 1000 THEN P2 = P2 + 1
        IF P1 = 1000 THEN P1 = 0
RETURN
```

The two arrays in the program, R1 and R2, function similarly to Vernam's two punched paper tapes. That is, they contain sequences of 1,000 and 999 random numbers, respectively. You can perform a modulo addition operation on the numbers in the two sequences and rotate the relationship between the numbers in each sequence to generate a new random number sequence.

After you enter your "secret" code, it is assigned to the string variable CODE$, similar to the previously developed RANDOM3.BAS program. The subroutine SETUP is then invoked. This subroutine obtains a position in a random number sequence similar to the previously developed routine of the same name. However, this routine uses the ASCII value of the "secret" code to obtain two different seed numbers and the location for the extraction of random numbers from each seed.

The first seed, specified by the variable SEED1, has its value determined by first multiplying the ASCII value of the first and third characters in the "secret" code. This produces a maximum value of 127 * 127, or 16,129. Because the number of seeds supported by BASIC is considerably higher, you then extract the ASCII value of the fifth character in the "secret" code and continuously divide it by 2 until it is less than or equal to 4. This results in the extension of the seed to a maximum value of 64,516. At this point, the value of a second seed is computed. First, the ASCII values of the second and fourth characters in the "secret" code are multiplied by one another. Then divide the ASCII value of the sixth character in the code by 2 until it is less than or equal to 4 and use that value as a multiplier of the product of the ASCII value of the second and fourth characters. Once the two seeds are computed, you are ready to select each seed and position yourself into the random number sequence in each seed prior to extracting the random numbers and placing them into the R1 and R2 arrays.

After the first seed is selected using the RANDOMIZE SEED1 statement, use a two-step approach to position yourself into the random number sequence within the selected seed. First multiply the ASCII values of the first, third, and fifth characters in the "secret" code to serve as the limit for the first FOR-NEXT loop, assigning the value of the three products to MAX. The ASCII value of the second character in the "secret" code is used as the stepping increment through the FOR-NEXT loop.

To go further into the random number sequence, use a second FOR-NEXT loop in which the ASCII value of the first character

multiplied by 500 serves as the limit of the loop, and the ASCII value of the third character in the "secret" code functions as the stepping mechanism through the loop. Once your positioning is completed, extract 1,000 random numbers, which are placed into the array R1.

Using the value computed for the second seed, use the statement RANDOMIZE SEED2 to select that seed. Next use the ASCII value of the characters in the "secret" code to position yourself into a random number sequence in that seed. Multiply the values of the second, fourth, and sixth characters in the "secret" code to serve as a limit for the FOR-NEXT loop and use the value of the fourth character to step through the loop. To go further into the sequence, another FOR-NEXT loop multiplies the ASCII value of the fourth character by 8,307 and uses the ASCII value of the second character as a mechanism to step through the loop. Then extract 999 random numbers and place them into the array R2.

When you examine the contents of the routine SETUP, note that both the ASCII value of the characters in the "secret" code word and the numerics entered in the program to govern the extraction process were used. You can use this subroutine as a guide to develop a random number extraction process that differs from the techniques presented in this book if you wish to obtain an additional degree of message security.

Once the subroutine SETUP is invoked, set the "paper tape" rotation scheme into operation by assigning the value 0 to the variable P1 and 1 to the variable P2. Then, for illustrative purposes, execute the subroutine ROTOR 500 times. If you were to use this subroutine to encipher a message, each time you invoked the subroutine, up to 999,000 times, you would receive a newly created random number whose value would be between 0 and 99. You must consider transmitting messages with less than 999,000 characters as well as the effect of adding a number with that possible variance to the set of values of plaintext characters you wish to encipher. For example, if 32 of the possible resulting character values are between 0 and 31, those enciphered characters become control characters that cannot be

transmitted over 7-bit electronic mail systems. Another concern you should think about is the necessity to print copies of enciphered messages (you cannot print control characters). You may wish to modify the ROTOR subroutine to produce random numbers within a range of values which, when added to the ASCII value of the supported set of plaintext characters, permits transmission over 7-bit electronic mail systems and the printing of enciphered messages.

The first statement in the subroutine ROTOR adds the random numbers in the arrays R1 (0) and R2 (1), multiplies the result by 100, performs a modulo 99 operation, and extracts the integer result. After the value of R is printed, the value of P1, which represents the position in the first random number sequence, is incremented by 1. Only after all 1,000 random numbers in the array R1 have been added using the first random number in R2 do you resequence or rotor the "paper tape." Here, when P1 equals 1,000, increment P2 by 1 and reset P1 to 0. Each time the subroutine ROTOR is invoked you continue this process.

To illustrate the result of the previously described set of routines, Listing 6.21 contains the random numbers generated from the execution of ROTOR.BAS. In this example the secret code ROUTE9 was used to generate the sequence of 500 random numbers generated by the program.

Listing 6.21. Execution of ROTOR.BAS using the secret code ROUTE9.

```
Enter your secret code (6 characters maximum) : ? ROUTE9
25 60 92 83 71 68 61 21 49 88 65 40 17 31 30  0  9 71 83 43 96
➥77 77 42 70 61 36
62 47 52 24 44  3  6 34 27 29 21 24 81 23 98 46 75 83 16 26 64
➥52 26 57  3 72 9
1 18 84 64 25 18 10 38 74 70 68 30 22 88 58 51 10  1 25 77 91  0
➥18 53 12 11 92
30  4 89 14 19 19 41 97 70 73 65 78 92 34 26 95 75 12 46  7 50
➥87 32 26 77 71 16
95 44 74 22 62  9  7 70  4 50 12 91 58 55 12 72 96 24 87 28  4
➥3 78 97 96 44 1
```

0 60 66 88 42 85 35 70 55   2 52 52 38 89   2 84 25   7 46 84 41 28
➡91 48 85 21 69
78 26 33 59 47 26 25 23 77   8   1 67 47   9 90 39 26   2 39 35 36
➡11 29 39 25 66 25
91 81 82 41 73 68 55 44 22 76 94 65 72   9 68 50 19 90 87 28   4
➡98   0 10 33 21 2
3   0 17 39 89 51 26 38 30 32 91 37 72 21 13 45 63 24 94 48 29 26
➡18 17 43 57 22
31 35 89 24 53 13 56 53 95 14 98 22 36 83 33   4 51 78 53 58 71
➡88 40 66 62 92 19
91 39 31 17 72 93 14 72 33 50 35 42 30 58 42 58   7 90 94 86 86
➡76 77 32 89 69 2
3 56 67 17 62 18 70 76   5 48 32 48 34 46 92 28 44 98 26 94 78 20
➡11 15 17 31 20
78 72 49 33 54 19 12 75 75 41 15 80 43 15 91 82 62   4   4 27   2
➡90 63 16 68 26 74
59 26   4   9 80 23 66 95 18 43 29 46 67   6 31   0 50 54 16 87 98
➡2 24 34 67 84 2
8 78 79 45 86 13 82 40   8 58 46 73 62 59 69 51   9   3 23 72 38 63
➡10 26 60 76 59
31 96 29 40 95 12 85 94 92 63 26   9 73 81 23 97 97 63 32 20 94
➡9 20 19 40 63 97
84 72   2   0 43 18 26 79 73 48 92 24 40 74 61   3 64 39 78 40 10
➡60 72   7 93 86 8
2 39 33 77 10 91   4 12 93 97 28 25 16 74 95 60 24 33 94 56 82 35
➡79 54 53 53 61
28 93 70 22 45 84   1 45 46 80 35 95 57 88 12 93 20 68   6 35

TOP SECRET

7

DEVELOPING PRACTICAL PROGRAMS

To conclude this book, this chapter discusses the utilization of previously developed subroutines and concepts into programs for enciphering and deciphering operations. Because you may prefer to use a ready-to-run set of enciphering and deciphering programs, this chapter also presents an overview of the use of a special pair of programs that are contained on the convenience disk that accompanies this book.

To refresh your memory, I have placed the sum of $1,000 with the publisher of this book as a reward to be given to the first person who correctly deciphers the enciphered message contained on the convenience disk. To illustrate the time value of information, this reward decreases by one dollar each day after the publication of this book. Thus, after three years, I will deem the value of the enciphered information as worthless and the reward offer will then terminate. The message and the procedure to claim the reward are described at the end of this chapter.

MODULE UTILIZATION

In previous chapters a number of subroutines were developed that performed predefined operations. Those programs were constructed based on the use of a number of subroutines that provided you with the capability to perform modular operations and link those operations together. You should consider using the previously developed series of subroutines and coding some of the concepts discussed in this book to modify those subroutines as a basis for developing programs to encipher and decipher messages to satisfy specific user requirements. You may require the use of an enciphering program, for example, that restricts the permissible range of enciphered characters. This restriction may result from the capability of an electronic mail system to only accept a limited character set or another limitation that affects the range of resulting enciphered characters. By tailoring previously developed routines you can create enciphering and deciphering programs to satisfy those requirements. To assist you in reviewing the functions performed by the subroutines developed and contained in this book, Table 7.1 summarizes their primary functions.

Table 7.1.
Subroutine Functionality.

Subroutine	Function Performed
INITIALIZE	This subroutine sets the elements in a string array to the uppercase letters of the alphabet.
FORMCIPHER	This subroutine forms a cipher alphabet by using an uppercase shift key character to rotate the plaintext alphabet until the shift key character is on the extreme right.
MSGENCIPHER	This subroutine converts plaintext to ciphertext using simple monoalphabetic substitution.

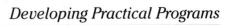
Subroutine	Function Performed
GROUPBY5	This subroutine prints a space after the display of each group of five enciphered characters.
MSGFILE	This subroutine assigns I/O files and accepts either keyboard or file input of messages.
CONVERTSTORE	This subroutine reads the contents of a plaintext message from a file, enciphers the message using a monoalphabetic substitution process, and outputs the resulting enciphered message to a file.
PRTOUT	This subroutine prints an enciphered message in groups of five characters, placing a space between each group and padding the last group with Xs until it contains five characters.
KEYWORD	This subroutine creates a keyword-based mixed alphabet based on a keyword or keyword phrase.
TRANSPORT	This subroutine creates a simple or numeric transposition mixed-sequence alphabet.
INTERVAL	This subroutine creates an interval extracted mixed alphabet.
MSGDCIPHER	This subroutine uses a mono-alphabetic substitution process to convert ciphertext to plaintext.
DMSGFILE	This subroutine is the reverse of the subroutine MSGFILE with respect to I/O file assignment names (this routine accepts files containing a ciphertext and assigns an output file to store plaintext).

continues

Table 7.1. Continued

Subroutine	Function Performed
DECIPHER	This routine can be considered as the reverse of the subroutine CONVERTSTORE because it converts ciphertext to plaintext.
DPRTOUT	This subroutine prints the resulting deciphered message on a line-by-line basis without character groupings.
DCONVERTSTORE	This subroutine can be considered as the reverse of the subroutine CONVERTSTORE because it converts ciphertext to plaintext.
RCONVERTSTORE	This is the modified version of the subroutine CONVERTSTORE used for random number-based encipherment. The subroutine smooths random numbers to between 0 and 25 for modulo 26 addition to alphabetic plaintext characters to produce enciphered text.
SETUP	This subroutine selects a random number seed and the location in the seed based on the ASCII value of the characters in a "secret" code.
RDCONVERTSTORE	This is the modified version of the subroutine CONVERTSTORE used for deciphering messages enciphered through the use of the subroutine RCONVERTSTORE.

THE ENCIPHER.EXE PROGRAM

Up to this point, the programs developed in this book contained significant restrictions concerning the character set available for encipherment. Most programs, for example, restricted the

composition of a message to the uppercase alphabet, forcing users to spell out punctuation characters such as COMMA for a "," and PERIOD or STOP to signify the end of a sentence.

Because you may prefer to type messages following a minimum of constraints, a new set of programs was developed to perform message enciphering and deciphering operations. This enciphering program is contained on the file ENCIPHER.EXE on your convenience disk in the form of a directly executable file. If you are curious as to why no source version of this program is provided, let your curiosity build for a few minutes—the rationale for providing only executable versions of the pair of programs described in this chapter will become apparent.

The ENCIPHER.EXE program was created using seven previously developed subroutines as a foundation for enciphering. Listing 7.1 contains the main module of ENCIPHER.BAS and illustrates the sequence in which different subroutines are called. The following examination of the coding used in several subroutines will provide you with the ability to modify one or more subroutines or use different groups of subroutines to tailor an enciphering program to your specific requirements. This will ensure that your program differs from this program, and it will make it much more difficult for someone to decipher a message. In fact, I recommend that you develop your own program rather than a program available for use by the general public—this is equivalent to one government providing a cipher machine to another government, especially if the latter is unfriendly. When this occurs, the unfriendly government uses the machine to attempt to decipher messages illicitly obtained by putting the machine through its paces, attempting one combination after another. The unfriendly government may also take the machine apart to determine what weaknesses exist and then attempt to exploit those weaknesses. Thus, not all of the subroutines in the program ENCIPHER.BAS are discussed in this chapter.

Listing 7.1. The main portion of the ENCIPHER.BAS program.

```
REM PROGRAM ENCIPHER.BAS
DIM PLAINTEXT$(128), CIPHERTEXT$(36, 92), KEY$(128)
      CLS
      PRINT "ENCIPHER>EXE PROGRAM enciphers text based on the use"
      PRINT "of enciphering techniques contained in the book TOP
      ➥SECRET:"
      PRINT "TRANSMITTING ELECTRONIC MAIL USING PRACTICAL ENCIPHERING
      ➥TECHNIQUES"
      PRINT
      PRINT "This program supports the use of upper- and lowercase
      ➥letters,"
      PRINT "digits, punctuation characters, and other characters
      ➥whose ASCII"
      PRINT "values range between 32 and 128, but EXCLUDES the use of
      ➥the"
      PRINT "forward slash (/), backslash (\) and double quote
      ➥characters."
      PRINT
      PRINT
AGN1:    INPUT "Enter your secret code (6 characters required) : ";
      ➥CODE$
      IF LEN(CODE$) = 6 THEN GOTO OK
      CLS
      PRINT "Your secret code must be 6 characters - please try again"
      PRINT
      GOTO AGN1
OK:   CLS
      GOSUB INITIALIZE            'initialize plaintext values
      GOSUB SETUP                 'obtain random seed and position in
                                  ➥seed
      GOSUB MSGFILE               'assign I/O files, place message on a
                                  ➥file
      GOSUB KEYWORD               'form keyword-based alphabet of 96
                                  ➥characters
      GOSUB PFORMCIPHER           'create 36 cipher alphabets
      GOSUB RCONVERTSTORE         'convert and store ciphertext on a file
      GOSUB PRTOUT                'print results
      STOP
```

The subroutine INITIALIZE was modified to expand the capability of ENCIPHER.BAS to accept a wider mixture of characters. The subroutine, whose coding is contained in Listing 7.2, was modified to initialize a string array labeled PLAINTEXT$ to all characters whose ASCII values are between 32 and 127, except those characters whose ASCII values equal 34, 47, and 92. The latter restriction eliminates the slash and backslash characters as well as the quote (") character from use in a message (the first two characters—the slash and the backslash—however, can be used to denote a message header or the end of a message). In addition, those characters whose ASCII values equal or exceed 128 or are below 32 should not be used in your plaintext message. ASCII characters whose values are below 32 are control characters that are either nonprintable or produce some strange effects such as horizontal and vertical tabs, form feeds, and so on. This can significantly alter the display of an enciphered message, and the exclusion of those characters enables an enciphered message to more easily be input through the keyboard if this should become necessary. ASCII characters whose values exceed 127 are known as extended ASCII characters. Because several popular electronic mail systems do not accept these characters, I have excluded their use in both the plaintext message and the resulting ciphertext. The resulting ciphertext is accomplished by structuring the creation of a modulo addition process that results in ciphertext characters whose ASCII values are between 32 and 127. In spite of these restrictions, the program opens up the vast majority of your keyboard for use in creating messages. You can use all uppercase and lowercase alphabetic characters, the space character, all digits, and most punctuation characters to prepare your message.

Listing 7.2. The modified subroutine INITIALIZE.

```
INITIALIZE:
    RESTORE
    REM Initialize plaintext values
    L = 0
    K = 32
```

continues

Listing 7.2. Continued

```
GOOD:      IF K = 47 OR K = 92 OR K = 34 THEN GOTO NOGD'skip \, / and "
       PLAINTEXT$(I) = CHR$(K)
       I = I + 1
NOGD:      K = K + 1
       IF I < 128 GOTO GOOD
RETURN
```

When you examine the statements in the modified subroutine
INITIALIZE, you may note that the variable I serves as the array
index and that the variable K serves as the ASCII character value.
When PLAINTEXT$(0)=CHR$(32), the 0 element of the string array
PLAINTEXT$ is set to a space character. Thus, the coding in Listing
7.2 replaces the READ and DATA statements used in previous
INITIALIZE subroutines.

Because the subroutine SETUP provides a mechanism to
select a random seed and positions you into a seed, I'll skip any
discussion of the code used in that subroutine (discussing the
mechanism used to obtain the seed and position within the seed
is similar to giving a burglar the keys to the store).

The code used in the subroutine KEYWORD is contained in
Listing 7.3. This subroutine is interesting because it uses the
"secret" code to develop a 30-character keyword. Note that the
expansion of the 6-character "secret" code to a 30-character
keyword substitutes the string "9" for the characters "\", "/",
and the double quote whose ASCII value is 34. To preclude any
extended ASCII characters occurring in the keyword, any character in the expansion process that has an ASCII value greater
than 127 is set to the string Q. The remaining modules in the
subroutine are similar to modules developed in the original
KEYWORD subroutine. The main difference between the remainder of the subroutines concerns the length of the array
PLAINTEXT$, which now contains 93 characters and has an ele-
ment value ranging from 0 to 92.

Listing 7.3. The KEYWORD subroutine.

```
KEYWORD:
      REM Place entered keyword into KEY$ array 1 character per
➥position
      REM but mix word through expansion to 30 characters
            MSGLEN = 30
            J = 1
            FOR I = 1 TO 6
AGN2:          IF J ?= 31 THEN GOTO NULLIT
               KEY$(J) = MID$(CODE$, I, 1)
               FOR J = J + 1 TO J + 4
               KEY$(J) = CHR$(ASC(MID$(CODE$, I, 1)) + ( J - 1))
               IF KEY$(J) = "\" OR KEY$(J) = "/" OR KEY$(J) =
➥CHR$(34) THEN KEY$(J) = "9"
               NEXT J
INCIT:             NEXT I
      REM ELIMINATE DUPLICATE LETTERS< REPLACE WITH CARRIAGE RETURNS
NULLIT:            K = 2
               FOR I = 1 TO MSGLEN
               FOR J = K TO MSGLEN
               IF KEY$(I) <> KEY$(J) GOTO NOTDUP
               KEY$(J) = CHR$(13)
NOTDUP:        NEXT J
               K = K + 1
               NEXT I
      REM REMOVE CARRIAGE RETURNS IN STRING
               X$ = ""
               FOR I = 1 TO MSGLEN
               IF KEY$(I) = CHR$(13) THEN GOTO ASKP
               X$ = X$ + KEY$(I)
ASKP:              NEXT I
      REM PLACE REVISED KEYWORD WITH NO DUPLICATE LETTERS BACK IN KEY$
               FOR I = 1 TO LEN(X$)
               KEY$(I) = MID$(X$, I, 1)
               NEXT I
      REM COMPARE KEY$ & PLAINTEXT$ ARRAYS, SET PLAINTEXT$ ELEMENT TO
➥CR WHEN MATCHED
```

continues

Listing 7.3. Continued

```
                    FOR J = 1 TO LEN(X$)
                    FOR K = 0 TO 92
                    IF KEY$(J) = PLAINTEXT$(K) THEN PLAINTEXT$(K) =
 ➡CHR$(13)
                    NEXT K
                    NEXT J
         REM CREATE ONE STRING
                    FOR I = 0 TO 92
                    IF PLAINTEXT$(I) = CHR$(13) THEN GOTO SKIP
                    X$ = X$ + PLAINTEXT$(I)
 SKIP:              NEXT I
         REM PLACE SEQUENCE BACK INTO PLAINTEXT$ ARRAY
                    FOR I = 0 TO 92
                    PLAINTEXT$(I) = MID$(X$, I + 1, 1)
                    NEXT I
 RETURN
```

Listing 7.4 contains the code found in the modified subroutine PFORMCIPHER. When you examine this subroutine you should note that it forms a two-dimensional ciphertext alphabet. The index JJ varies from 0 to 35 and forms 36 cipher alphabets that are based on the keyword exploded from the "secret" code. At this point, you may realize that ENCIPHER.BAS uses a combination of random numbers and a rotating ciphertext alphabet to perform encipherment. Exactly how this occurs is illustrated by the code in the modified subroutine RCONVERTSTORE.

Listing 7.4. The modified PFORMCIPHER subroutine.

```
 KEYWORD:
  PFORMCIPHER:
             REM routine to form 35 CIPHERTEXT alphabets based upon
 ➡the characters in the code
             FOR JJ = 0 TO 35
             FOR KK = 0 TO 92
             CIPHERTEXT$(JJ, KK) = PLAINTEXT$((KK + JJ) MOD 92)
```

```
        NEXT KK
        NEXT JJ
RETURN
```

Listing 7.5 contains the code in the modified subroutine RCONVERTSTORE. When you examine the code in the subroutine RCONVERTSTORE, note that after extracting a two-digit random number, X=INT(RND*100), the result is divided by 1.087 (use the integer portion of the result). This smooths the random number to a value between 0 and 92 (this corresponds to the 93 elements in the array PLAINTEXT$). Now compare each character in each line of the plaintext to a character in the array PLAINTEXT$. When a match occurs, add the index value of the match position in PLAINTEXT$ to the smoothed value of X using MOD 92 addition. The result, stored in the variable z, is used to extract a character from one of the ciphertext alphabets contained in the string array CIPHERTEXT$. Thus, ENCIPHER.BAS uses random numbers to extract characters from a two-dimensional alphabet to obtain enciphered text. The routines used for enciphering illustrate how you can combine two or more techniques to develop your own enciphering program.

Listing 7.5. The modified RCONVERTSTORE subroutine.

```
RCONVERTSTORE:
    REM Routine to convert and store ciphertext on a file
    OPEN INFILE$ FOR INPUT AS #1
    OPEN OUTFILE$ FOR OUTPUT AS #2
    ALPHA = 0       'first alphabetic pointer
    PRINT "Enciphering operation in progress ";
    DO UNTIL EOF(1)
        INPUT #1, TEXT$
        PRINT ".";
        MSGLEN = LEN(TEXT$)
        IF MID$(TEXT$, 1, 1) = "/" THEN GOTO CLEARTXT1
        IF MID$(TEXT$, 1, 1) = "\" THEN GOTO DONE2
        REM Convert plaintext to ciphertext
            FOR I = 1 TO MSGLEN
            X = INT(RND * 100)        'get 2 digit integer
```

continues

Listing 7.5. Continued

```
                    X = INT(X / 1.087)          'smooth to 0 to 92
                    FOR J = 0 TO 92
                    IF MID$(TEXT$, I, 1) = CIPHERTEXT$(ALPHA, Z) THEN
➡GOTO MATCH
                    NEXT J
MATCH:                  Z = ( KJ + X) MOD 92
                    MID$(TEXT$, I, 1) = CIPHERTEXT$(ALPHA, Z)
                    NEXT I
                    ALPHA = ALPHA + 1
                    IF ALPHA = 35 THEN ALPHA = 0 'reset alphabet
➡pointer
CLEARTXT1:          WRITE #2, TEXT$
     LOOP
DONE2:          CLOSE #2
          CLOSE #1
RETURN
```

The execution of the program ENCIPHER.EXE is illustrated in Listings 7.6 through 7.8. Listing 7.6 illustrates the display of the first screen of the program that displays information about the program and then prompts you to enter a six-digit "secret" code. Unlike the restrictions on the plaintext characters in a message, the code can consist of most characters in the ASCII character set; however, as discussed in this book, you should select a code that is not difficult to repeat (I recommend the use of printable characters).

Listing 7.6. The first screen display of the ENCIPHER.EXE program.

```
ENCIPHER.EXE PROGRAM enciphers text based on the use
of enciphering techniques contained in the book TOP SECRET:
TRANSMITTING ELECTRONIC MAIL USING PRACTICAL ENCIPHERING
TECHNIQUES

This program supports the use of upper- and lowercase letters,
digits, punctuation characters, and other characters whose ASCII
```

```
values range between 32 and 128, but EXCLUDES the use of the
forward slash (/), backslash (\) and double quote characters.

Enter your secret code (6 characters required) : ? TESTME
```

Listing 7.7 illustrates the second screen displayed when the program ENCIPHER.EXE is executed. This screen first displays information concerning the filenames used to store the plaintext and ciphertext messages. Because the keyboard is selected for entering the plaintext message, the program then displays information concerning the use of the slash and backslash characters. As in the previously developed programs, the slash is used to prefix headers that should remain as plaintext, and the backslash is used to indicate the termination of the message.

Listing 7.7. The second screen displayed upon execution of ENCIPHER.EXE.

```
Enter filename to store plaintext message, default=MESSAGE.DAT  :
Enter filename to store enciphered message, default=CIPHERTX.DAT :
Select keyboard (k) or file (f) message input: K
Enter your message - place a / at the beginning of each line
that should remain in plaintext and a \ on a separate line
to indicate the end of the enciphered message

/TO JIMMY K. ESTES III
/OFFICE MANAGER
/THE WHITE HOUSE
It has come to my attention that we must develop a plan for
moving all personal furnishing out of this building as soon
as possible.  The latest poll suggests our days are numbered.
Please prepare the plan and transmit it to me using the cipher
code we previously agreed to use for information of this type.
Your budget for moving is restricted to $123,456.12.
\
Enciphering operation in progress .........
Press Return key to display resulting enciphered message
```

After the previously discussed information is displayed, you can enter your message. After the backslash character is entered the program displays the message "Enciphering operation in progress . . . ." Because the program can require from a few seconds to half a minute or more depending upon the computer you use to encipher your message, dots are displayed while the program executes so you know it is working. Once the encipherment operation is completed the message "Press Return key to display resulting enciphered message" is displayed. Once you press the Return key, the resulting enciphered message is displayed as illustrated in Listing 7.8. The enciphered message is also written onto the file CIPHERTX.DAT so you can transfer that file through a communications program.

Listing 7.8. The enciphered message created by ENCIPHER.BAS.

```
Resulting enciphered message is:


TO JIMMY K. ESTES III
OFFICE MANAGER
THE WHITE HOUSE
5V3~3:C-0RCs_(XX&UATiSZ¦]kNSosyCM>X^x,:zk[8fOVz7=pO[ofl¦F )
CxbfK_;49YU<_m#t.'q[&_jAoek3Pxr4zcQ$Me$'suF+Z00U[2xlpx¦0{y;
[.}]P_{SY:}GLYGcv=H0Uz^#r$7!^<]~Co%1c^AINt@&#tLRmpIeXfYv+?_Q
YwN(JBr@'Q@FgTsguZD;3qgYa#zr<0W7xv;.G:dWP7HXF6)zgOW3gC2,R=+#%i
;;+&z?Xway RTZNh9JIDriv)LmO[%U5i,w,>9NQ:5ITQ8ySH>*,S'(#8<U~b~I
12dx:AIC$m{9Cgi_axS8[s#]a<d +CS<)kn_h>6q,KU_'$}$2^RT
```

THE DECIPHER.EXE PROGRAM

Similar to the ENCIPHER.EXE program, the DECIPHER.EXE program operates through the use of three screens. The execution of DECIPHER.EXE is illustrated in Listings 7.9 through 7.11.

To illustrate the use of the deciphering program, use the program to operate on the previously enciphered message

contained on the file CIPHERTX.DAT. Listing 7.9 illustrates the entry of the same "secret" code that was used to encipher the previously created plaintext message.

Listing 7.9. The first screen displayed upon execution of DECIPHER.EXE.

```
DECIPHER.EXE PROGRAM deciphers text based on the use
of enciphering techniques contained in the book TOP SECRET:
TRANSMITTING ELECTRONIC MAIL USING PRACTICAL ENCIPHERING TECHNIQUES

This programs supports the use of upper- and lowercase letters,
digits, punctuation characters, and other characters whose ASCII
values range between 32 and 128, but EXCLUDES the use of the
forward slash (/), backslash (\) and double quote characters.

Enter your secret code (6 characters required) : ? TESTME
```

Once your "secret" code is entered, the program displays a second screen which, like ENCIPHER.EXE, enables you to assign filenames for storing the plaintext and enciphered messages and select keyboard or file input (see Listing 7.10). In this example, the default filenames are accepted, and when the deciphering operation commences, an appropriate message is displayed. After the deciphering operation is completed and you press Return, the resulting deciphered message is displayed (see Listing 7.11). When you compare the plaintext message in Listing 7.7 to the deciphered message contained in Listing 7.11 you should note they are exactly the same.

Listing 7.10. The second screen displayed upon execution of DECIPHER.EXE.

```
Enter filename to store plaintext message, default=MESSAGE.DAT
Enter filename for enciphered message, default=CIPHERTX.DAT
Select keyboard (k) or file (f) message input: F
Deciphering operation in progress ..........
Press Return key to display resulting deciphered message
```

Listing 7.11. Resulting deciphered message.

```
Resulting deciphered message is:

TO JIMMY K. ESTES III
OFFICE MANAGER
THE WHITE HOUSE
It has come to my attention that we must develop a plan for
moving all personal furnishing out of this building as soon
as possible. The latest poll suggests our days are numbered.
Please prepare the plan and transmit it to me using the cipher
code we previously agreed to use for information of this type.
Your budget for moving is restricted to $123,456.12.
```

THE CHALLENGE

To conclude this book, an enciphered message is presented in Listing 7.12. Unlike the task faced by most cryptanalysts that do not have access to an enciphering system used to create a message, I have considerably simplified the task of deciphering this message. This message was enciphered using the directly executable program ENCIPHER.EXE, which is contained on the convenience disk. The enciphered message, stored on the file SECRET.MSG on the convenience disk, can be deciphered using the directly executable program DECIPHER.EXE, which is also contained on the disk SECRET.MSG accompanying this book.

Listing 7.12. The "challenge" message.

```
/TO: ZONE MANAGERS
/FROM: CORPORATE QUALITY CONTROL
RT m,q>>EA5;uSLxo6W0Cy¦&fHkf,1.8{Nhx)v~3K)O`;PHK`Q21)`D#bnFvweB6l
aZ@pk;N<x^1=qg^Hx8=q%pX4}e~X<N*2*@T2I=$fQqR?pAK*kb*6@2wM7Xhls36b
iYfAz]8sk~c]8+J8v:RGUlg19;S{ZMA&gxoymv;d#+1#Oeo+@%,w;-2vH^dE.TDwMg{
:Z}Z7&J{R$usy(I1lBG[EHGCV$mywR6`MnI5:v'?Enl1<QVJ<kDLP-SFvZ]}Iz`bB{=9
QDU)¦dFqUTpesb k[C[d?eIr _Ansu(yqNJQE*XFb'fIazV>H]¦g#rgeve@8.3'I0?6
w8D}{mAPP¦y3KYsf6QzMUG`YIh1*)9&?FD4l*u5ckeF^7<n9d;%ROp%NDKKmS9Y7+l^`
```

```
*XLB7^?UMCuW`&*x.q{66jg# >xl2U2%>)[7BH~iP8¦j%[>ln(o,3o4cBxy)6[gr
Dy''dm#}3a2F^[
```

Providing the deciphering program may simplify the task of deciphering the message. You can consider using a trial-and-error approach by using different "secret" codes in an attempt to decipher the message. As you cycle through various combinations of "secret" codes, one of the points raised a number of times in this book should become apparent: the program provides a level of privacy for electronic transmission that deters the casual observer of a message from understanding the contents of the message.

The reason for providing only directly executable copies of the two programs whose use was described in this chapter is to hide the technique employed to use the "secret" code used by the enciphering program to generate a random number sequence. Although I have left the door unlocked, I will not turn on the lights!

If you feel you are successful in deciphering the message illustrated in Listing 7.12 and contained on the file SECRET.MSG, please send a description of the approach you used to decipher the message, the type of computer you used, and any coding you wrote, as well as the deciphered message, to:

Assistant to the Publisher, Sams Publishing
Prentice Hall Computer Publishing
11711 North College Avenue
Carmel, Indiana 46032

At the present time I am considering writing a second edition of this book. This second edition is planned to expand on the contents of this book to include automation techniques used by cryptanalysts. I would like to consider describing the techniques

you used to decipher the message illustrated in Listing 7.12 (or even approaches you took that were not successful). I welcome all comments concerning the challenge message and all aspects of this book. All submissions will be considered for inclusion (with permission) in the next edition of this book.

TOP SECRET

CONVENIENCE DISK FILES

A

This appendix lists the name of each file contained on the convenience disk and a description of the function of each file. To obtain additional information concerning the operation and utilization of each program, refer to the files listed in this appendix in the order in which they are described in each chapter. Some files, such as those whose names end with the extension .EXE, are executable versions of BASIC programs. Although .EXE files are not listed in this book because they represent executable versions of .BAS programs, the chapter in which the BASIC program is described is used as the chapter reference.

Chapter	Filename	Description
2	SHIFT.BAS	This program creates a sequence of shifted alphabets.
	SHIFT.EXE	This file is the executable version of SHIFT.BAS.
	CIPHER1.BAS	This program creates a shifted alphabet based on the entry of an alphabetic shift key character.

continues

Chapter	Filename	Description
	CIPHER1.EXE	This file is the executable version of CIPHER1.BAS.
	CIPHER2.BAS	This program enciphers a one-line message using a cipher alphabet formed by shifting the plaintext alphabet through the use of an alphabetic shift key.
	CIPHER2.EXE	This file is the executable version of CIPHER2.BAS.
	CIPHER3.BAS	This program expands on the functionality of CIPHER2.BAS by adding a routine that displays the resulting enciphered text in groups of five characters.
	CIPHER3.EXE	This file is the executable version of CIPHER3.BAS.
	CIPHER4.BAS	This program expands on the functionality of CIPHER3.BAS by permitting spaces between words in a plaintext message and selectively enciphering the message using a simple monoalphabetic substitution process.
	CIPHER4.EXE	This file is the executable version of CIPHER4.BAS.
	DCIPHER4.BAS	This program deciphers a message previously enciphered through the use of CIPHER4.BAS.
	DCIPHER4.EXE	This file is the executable version of DCIPHER4.BAS.

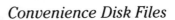 

Chapter	Filename	Description
3	WORD.BAS	This program develops an alphabet based on the entry of a keyword or keyword phrase.
	WORD.EXE	This file is the executable version of WORD.BAS.
	CIPHER5.BAS	This program enciphers a message based on the use of a keyword or keyword phrase and an alphabetic shift key using a mono-alphabetic substitution process.
	CIPHER5.EXE	This file is the executable version of CIPHER5.BAS.
	DCIPHER5.BAS	This program deciphers a message enciphered using the program CIPHER5.BAS.
	DCIPHER5.EXE	This file is the executable version of DCIPHER5.BAS.
4	CIPHERTR.BAS	This program enciphers a message using a transposition matrix and a mono-alphabetic substitution process based on a keyword or keyword phrase and an alphabetic shift key. This program displays the composition of different alphabets to illustrate the operation of the enciphering process.
	CIPHERTR.EXE	This file is the executable version of CIPHERTR.BAS.

continues

Chapter	Filename	Description
	CIPHER6.BAS	This program adds an interval extraction capability to CIPHERTR.BAS.
	CIPHER6.EXE	This file is the directly executable version of CIPHER6.BAS.
	DCIPHER6.BAS	This program deciphers messages enciphered using the program CIPHER6.BAS.
	DCIPHER6.EXE	This file is the directly executable version of DCIPHER6.BAS.
5	POLY1.BAS	This program creates a Vigenére tableau.
	POLY1.EXE	This file is the directly executable version of POLY1.BAS.
	POLY2.BAS	This program enciphers a message based on the use of two keywords or keyword phrases using a poly-alphabetic substitution process and 26 cipher alphabets.
	POLY2.EXE	This file is the directly executable version of POLY2.BAS.
	DPOLY2.BAS	This program deciphers messages previously enciphered using the program POLY2.BAS.
	DPOLY2.EXE	This file is the directly executable version of DPOLY2.BAS.
6	RANDOM1.BAS	This program generates random numbers between 0 and 25.

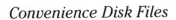 

Chapter	Filename	Description
	RANDOM1.EXE	This file is the directly executable version of RANDOM1.BAS.
	RANDOM2.BAS	This program demonstrates the use of random numbers to encipher a one-line message.
	RANDOM2.EXE	This file is the directly executable version of RANDOM2.BAS.
	DRANDOM2.BAS	This program deciphers a one-line message previously enciphered using the program RANDOM2.BAS.
	DRANDOM2.EXE	This file is the directly executable version of DRANDOM2.BAS.
	POSITION.BAS	This program demonstrates the positioning to a place in the BASIC random number generator based on a "secret" code up to six characters in length.
	POSITION.EXE	This file is the directly executable version of POSITION.BAS.
	ROTOR.BAS	This program constructs a new random number sequence based on the extraction of random numbers from the seeds.
	ROTOR.EXE	This file is the directly executable version of ROTOR.BAS.

continues

Chapter	Filename	Description
	RTEST.BAS	This program scans a random number seed to locate any sequence of five repeated numbers.
	RANDOM3.BAS	This program enciphers messages using the BASIC random number generator and a six-position "secret" code to locate a starting point in the random number generator.
	RANDOM3.EXE	This file is the directly executable version of RANDOM3.BAS.
	DRANDOM3.BAS	This program deciphers messages previously enciphered using the program RANDOM3.BAS.
	DRANDOM3.EXE	This file is the directly executable version of DRANDOM3.BAS.

INDEX

Q-R

W-Z

DISK INFORMATION

The disk included with this book contains the example programs discussed in the book. Most of the programs are included as BASIC text files (*.BAS) and executable programs (*.EXE).

The SECRET.MSG file contains a special encrypted message—if you're the first to break the code, you could win $1,000!

INSTALLATION

The software on the included disk is stored in a compressed form. You must follow this installation procedure before you can use the software:

1. From a DOS prompt, set your default drive to the drive that contains the installation disk. For example, if the floppy disk is in drive A:, type A: and press Enter.
2. Type INSTALL *drive* (where *drive* is the drive letter of your hard drive) and press Enter. For example, to copy the programs to your C: drive, type INSTALL C: and press Enter.

This procedure installs all the files to a directory called \SECRET! on your hard drive. To install the files, you need at least 1.2 megabytes of free space on your hard drive.

By opening this package, you are agreeing to be bound by the following agreement: